Advanced Praise for
Fort Unicorn and the Duchess of Knothing

"Of the many books I've read about mental illness, addiction, and a mother's love, this is the most powerful. It grabbed my heart and left an indelible footprint there."

—Jill Muehrcke
Editor, NONPROFIT WORLD
Owner, JP Publications

"This memoir is at once spare, raw, heartbreaking and lovely. The stories are unique, yet familiar, for anyone impacted by substance use disorder which, at this point, is all of us. *Fort Unicorn* is a gift to the world, because it reminds us of the humanity in every person struggling with addiction."

—Nora Hertel
Journalist and the founder of *The Optimist*,
a digital news startup in Minnesota

"A must read for all who are touched by anyone struggling with addiction, mental illness, or homelessness. During my 25+ years working law enforcement in the San Diego area, I've witnessed personally the tragic and often grisly consequences of these sad realities; issues too often closeted by shame, and they needn't be. This heartbreaking memoir offers an intimate window into losing a loved one to their demons, and what it means to love unconditionally."

—Lisa Stinson (Officer Lisa Civulka Turner)
Retired law enforcement
CA Highway patrol
University of California San Diego Police Department
City of Coronado Police Department

"I met Andrea Nelson through boxing and was impressed by her forthrightness and courage. She has now summoned a different—far greater—kind of courage and written a candid and heartbreaking memoir of her doomed effort to save her beloved daughter, Shyloh, from the demons that so haunted her. It's a moving story that will resonate deeply with anyone who has experienced loss, which, of course, is all of us."

—Doug Moe
Journalist and author of *The Right Thing to Do: Kit Saunders-Nordeen and the Rise of Women's Intercollegiate Athletics at the University of Wisconsin and Beyond*

"Nelson invites the reader to see the unhoused through the lens of love and acceptance, not judgement or distaste. Her candid description of struggling to accept her daughter's decisions to live as she chose will help others facing difficulties accepting their loved ones' choices. One of the hardest parts of loving someone with addiction and/or mental illness is the need to give up trying to control their journey.

If you have struggled with where to draw the boundary between supporting and saving your loved one, read this, and you will know that you are not alone."

—Robin Monson-Dupuis LCSW SAC RYT
Author of *Spirit Son: A Mother's Journey to Reconnect with Her Son After His Death from Heroin Overdose*

"This book is long overdue in being written; sadly, *Fort Unicorn* is a too common yet unfamiliar story. I thank the author for her courage in sharing this story. I hope it touches and transforms the reader."

—Kathy Krueger, M.A. LMFT
Psychotherapist
Certified EMDR Therapist
EMDRIA Approved Consultant

"In her memoir, *Fort Unicorn and the Duchess of Knothing*, Andrea Nelson has provided her readers with an authentic and heartfelt journey into both her life and her daughter, Shyloh's, life.

As a mother and woman in long term recovery, I was so deeply moved by the painful and passionate relationship between mother & daughter—the struggles between detachment, rescuing, enabling, how to save your child, set boundaries and honor her path. The progression of this tragic disease is reflected in the author's honest dialogue. I literally could not put this book down.

Shyloh was a Mentor at Connections Counseling and touched so many of our lives deeply. Her memory lives on in our hearts."

—Shelly Dutch, CSAC
Founder of Connections Counseling
Founder of Recovery Foundation
Co-Founder of Horizon High School

"In *Fort Unicorn and the Duchess of Knothing*, Andrea Nelson traces the tragic path of her effervescent, talented, and deeply troubled daughter. In so doing, Nelson confronts the relentlessness of addiction, the parallel universe of the unhoused, the complexity of mental illness, and the profound agony of love. This is a book of devastating immediacy and acute compassion—a book that can better the world."

—Nathan Jandl, PhD
Founding editor, Edge Effects
Assistant Director of Sustainability, UW–Madison

"The heartrending story told in *Fort Unicorn* resonates, compelling me to reframe the way I deal with adversity in my own life. Andrea offers a lesson of perspective and courage, and of how to be conscious of the silent struggles in the world."

—Mike Noack
Chief Growth Officer & co-founder, Blue Lake Consulting Group
boxer and friend

"It might be tempting to put off reading this small book, but you will miss a remarkable opportunity if you do. This memoir is a beautifully written doorway into what it means to love, as well as a meditation on finding compassion for those in our community who have been cast aside. Clear, honest and concise, *Fort Unicorn* unflinchingly details the power of letting go to stay close. It is an uncompromising and nuanced gift to the world."

—Jennifer Smith
Dedicated reader, former editor, lifelong friend

"Painful to read...but need to read if you have not personally experienced losing your child to the agonizing struggle of addiction but want to understand."

—Anonymous, a mourning father of a beloved son lost to heroin

"Those of us who have seen addiction and mental health struggles close-up in our loved ones will develop fresh insight from Andrea Nelson's memoir. It will help many develop fresh compassion for themselves through knowing that they are not alone in their grief. She helps us understand that bearing witness to such suffering is the practice that makes us ready for the hardest moments of life."

—Dennis Boyer, disabled veterans advocate, author

"Andrea Nelson has written a poignant and moving memoir, about freedom, loss, courage and unconditional love. In *Fort Unicorn and the Duchess of Knothing*, Andrea takes us on a journey onto the streets of San Diego, where her daughter, Shyloh, descends deeper into mental illness and addiction, a world void of societal rules and limits. The author shares her own feelings of madness, anger, confusion, and pain, driven by love to find her daughter and bring her home. She walks us through the fragile veil between stability and illness and shows us these two worlds are not as different as they may appear.

—Troy Gosz, Co-Founder of FLYY
(Forward Learning Youth and Young Adults)

"This story reminds us that we are not alone, that love comes in all forms, and there is not one 'right' way to show up for one another and ourselves. We are honored and humbled to write a review for this beautiful and important memoir."

—Jessi Kushner, Co-Founder of FLYY; Founder of Collective Voices

"Our nation's failure to prioritize and adequately help adult children afflicted by the often-deadly combination of mental illness, addiction, and homelessness is a disgrace. Andrea, with the mental and physical stamina of a professional athlete, was valiant in her many attempts to rescue her daughter, Shyloh. No child should have to suffer like this, and no parent should have to endure the horror of viewing their deceased child's body. One hopes that Shyloh felt her mother's ever-present and deep love and that Andrea moves forward with courage, hope, and the memories of her precious Shyloh. Andrea's resourcefulness and tireless bravery will inspire all parents who are fighting to literally keep their children alive."

—Donna Weikert, child custody mediator

Andrea Nelson has achieved something brilliant in *Fort Unicorn*. With honesty and beauty, she weaves the ache of a mother's grief with the joy of being blessed by the life of her daughter, Shyloh. This is a must-read for anyone who has experienced addiction loss and those of us who work with people in recovery. Addiction loss does not discriminate and can impact anyone.

—Caroline Beidler, MSW, author of
*Downstairs Church: Finding Hope in the Grit
of Addiction and Trauma Recovery*

Fort Unicorn & the Duchess of Knothing:

A Mother's Fight To Save Her Daughter

ANDREA NELSON

www.ten16press.com - Waukesha, WI

Author's note: The experiences in this book are all true, as far as personal memory allows. I have done my best to share our mother-daughter journey with love, respect, and integrity. To remain faithful to our relationship and our voices, all written communication—personal and public—will appear with profanity and errors intact. To revise them would have destroyed authenticity, something my daughter would have deplored.

Sam,
Thank you
for sharing this
journey with
me.

For you, Shyloh. Loving you always.
- your Mamabear

CONTENTS

Life is a stubborn return from sorrow again and again. To suffer longing and loss makes you not a victim but a human being.

– from *Drawing Life* by David Gelernter

THE GUEST HOUSE - by Rumi

This being human is a guest house.
Every morning a new arrival.

A joy, a depression, a meanness,
some momentary awareness comes
as an unexpected visitor.

Welcome and entertain them all!
Even if they're a crowd of sorrows,
who violently sweep your house
empty of its furniture,
still, treat each guest honorably.
He may be clearing you out
for some new delight.

The dark thought, the shame, the malice,
meet them at the door laughing,
and invite them in.

Be grateful for whoever comes,
because each has been sent
as a guide from beyond.

THE WAY IT IS - by William Stafford

There's a thread you follow. It goes among
things that change. But it doesn't change.
People wonder about what you are pursuing.
You have to explain about the thread.
But it is hard for others to see.
While you hold it you can't get lost.
Tragedies happen; people get hurt
or die; and you suffer and get old.
Nothing you do can stop time's unfolding.
You don't ever let go of the thread.

FOREWORD

When I first met Andrea Nelson, I knew she had a story to tell. It just wasn't the story I was expecting.

She was setting up a boxing ring, preparing for a tournament she organized. I wrote a newspaper article about the fights, and I knew instantly that this woman, this former professional boxer who loved gardening, going barefoot, and talking about great literature, needed to be featured in a book I was writing at the time. She was, and each time I talked to her, I drew from her unfathomably deep well of experiences. The thing about Andrea is that you are never really done knowing her. You are never finished learning about her, and her life. The next time I see her, she could begin a story with, "This was when I was working as a cartographer in the Amazon..." or, "Back when I was an astronaut..." and I wouldn't even bat an eye. When we gather with our families for dinner, she might make an offhand comment about "that bear I fought." With Andrea, anything is possible.

But amidst her exciting adventures, her true story, the one with the most meaning, brimming with uncommon joy and tremendous sorrow, was hiding in plain sight. A few years ago, when we were first getting to know each other, I saw a flyer she had posted. It said she was looking for her daughter. Shyloh, whose resemblance to her mother was uncanny, was missing. Eventually, I realized that this – Andrea's search for her daughter – was her real story. This was her journey. Everything else, no matter how exciting it seemed, was merely an aside or a footnote, as she pursued her one true love.

The problem, of course, is that Shyloh was not an easy person to find. Beauty never is. When we go on a quest for truth or meaning or love, we're chasing a moving and mysterious target. Shyloh was no different, both literally and figuratively. She was always moving, in a geographical sense, but she was also always changing, sometimes dramatically, and her mental illness, drug addiction, and powerful aversion to a cage of any kind made her nearly impossible to find, and completely impossible to hold onto.

In the spring of 2021, Andrea told me she wanted to write a book about her daughter. She asked if she could send pages as she worked on them. In her initial message, she ended with these words: "I'm anxious to hear what you have to say."

The rest of the year was a barrage of stories: maddening, sickening stories of a mother who would literally fly across the country and wander, on foot, through homeless encampments looking for her daughter. It was the kind of stuff that made you gnash your teeth and grasp at your gut.

I read all the stories myriad times, sending back notes and minor edits, as Andrea's tales gradually turned into a coherent book.

She told me, at the outset, that she was sick of artificial happy endings. She said she wanted to write something true, and the truth was that her daughter was suffering beyond measure, and there would be no happy ending.

Andrea hated when I pointed this out, but Shyloh's story was not entirely tragic. Her defining characteristics were humor, whimsy and creativity. She turned everything she touched into art, and she seemed, at times, to be on a grand adventure. The trail Andrea followed, as she searched for her daughter, was one of beautiful artwork, of forts and heroes and villains and jokes and strange imaginings. Shyloh's life was a trail of bright colors and fanciful wordplay, of buried treasure and sinister monsters.

And then, one day, I woke up and received a text message from Andrea informing me that the trail had stopped. Shyloh had died, in a tent, in California.

A few weeks later, I attended a memorial service for a young woman I had never met in real life, yet seemed to know her far better than many, perhaps most, of the other people whose funerals I've attended. I had been reading, and re-reading, her life, over and over again.

With Shyloh's death, her mother's search did not end. It merely changed. She had spent years looking for Shyloh in alleys, city parks, and under bridges, on the margins of society. Now, with Shyloh's body laid to rest, Andrea continued her search. Only she went deeper, further into her daughter's life, which is so like the countless lives of the unhoused, the addicted, and the mentally ill. People often say they are invisible, hidden outside of our society and outside of our comfortable lives. *Fort Unicorn and the Duchess of Knothing* shows us that some things are worth looking for, worth searching for, worth seeing, in all their complicated beauty, even if it means striking out on an uncomfortable journey.

Andrea stayed true to her promise not to tack on a happy ending or hollow lesson. But the sadness of the book you hold in your hands does not detract from its beauty, nor from the beauty of the young woman it is about. Things can be horrible and beautiful at the same time, and Shyloh's story – and her mother's journey – stand as proof. This is one of the most meaningful, important books you will ever read. Andrea and Shyloh were closer than the vast majority of parents and children. They were inexorably linked. They still are. Even so, Andrea understood that we must actively seek out the things we love each day, and we can never expect them to come looking for us. Imagine if great painters of old didn't set out on their searches for sunflowers and angels and gods.

When you read this book, you will cry many times. You will shake your fists at inept and uncaring social networks, and you will laugh, several times, at how funny life can be. When you are done reading it (and you will certainly not be able to put it down), you will go out, and search, with new vision and purpose, for the beautiful, meaningful, fleeting people and ideas that deserve to be found in our shared world. They can't always be held onto, or saved forever, but they are real, and they are worth finding. You will know that everyone has a story to tell, and it's not always the story we were expecting.

—*Matt Geiger*
Author and journalist

INTRODUCTION

July 2019 Spring Valley, California

When I first walk into my daughter's encampment, I'm both horrified by the situation and impressed by her resourcefulness. Hidden within these bushes and utilizing the overhanging branches to tie up tarps and tent peaks, Shyloh has made herself a wall-less "house." I don't know how much of what is here was here before her and I forget to ask, but her handiwork is clearly everywhere. A worn loveseat and chair, with umbrellas imaginatively tied above for shade serves as her living room. Her bedroom, tucked away beneath a small olive tree, is a tiny one-person tent with a tattered parasol tied at the peak to keep out the rain. Her bed is a comfy blanket which she shares with a giant stuffed giraffe, found and lovingly named Raffie. Another larger, equally tattered tent is her sitting room, furnished with bike parts, skateboards, a couple camp chairs and an assortment of other treasures.

A cooler sits in another shady spot serving as a fridge, wrapped in a tarp secured with a complex of bungee cords to ward off the ants she's constantly battling. A crafting area (of course!) on a large wooden spool, and several small and elaborately decorated displays here and there, almost like shrines, ornamented with little finds and creations. And except for the fringe of garbage, what looks like years' worth of built-up human castoffs, the huge piles of filthy, nearly rotting clothes, food containers, bike parts, old electronics, it could be a kid's fort in a desert thicket.

She's named her space Fort Unicorn, and she, the Duchess of Knothing. The initials *FU* are her own private joke, a subtle curse against the world, and I note her chosen play on words spelling Nothing with a "K." My reality feels fractured, but I smile inwardly despite this; these names suit her in this place.

She was little more than a flutter in my belly when I overheard the name Shilo in a conversation and decided that's what I'd name her. She would be my first child and my first true love, absolute and unconditional. I chose to spell it "Shyloh," imagining the beautiful flourishes those long elegant letters would offer. For decades she and I would elaborately draw her name, playing with the swirls and swoops, adding flowers and butterflies and vines. The name fit her. She too was elaborate and beautiful.

November 2020 San Diego, California

"It's Grace!" she corrects again with a snarl. I tell her I'm sorry, I keep forgetting, but in truth I'm resisting the name.

My daughter and I are together again, now under an overpass in San Diego. Shyloh shows me her new graffiti tag, "ASF," which she's spray-painted in creative and colorful flair on the graffiti-covered concrete around us. Short for "As Fuck," as in: dope as fuck, high as fuck, hungry as fuck, sad as fuck, lonely as fuck. She tells me she'd noticed that the letters ASF looked like the word ACE and decided to make *Ace* her street name. This eventually morphed into the name *Grace*.

When I decided I needed to tell Shyloh's story, I imagined I was speaking for her alone. I soon recognized this is as much my story as it is hers. This writing has been cathartic, but also terribly draining. I feel my feet dragging when reaching another point in the journey that needs to be revisited before it can be put into words on paper. Memories are etched into my very being, of swaying to James Taylor's "You've Got a Friend" blasting on my living room stereo, Shyloh tucked safely away inside my beach ball belly, of the first time I held her in my arms, the smell of her, the maternal ache as she nursed. I remember anxiously letting go of the bicycle seat as she successfully pedaled, wobbled, solo across the yard for the first time. Of sending her off to her first day of school, my eager anticipation for the few afternoon hours to myself, and the alarming realization that I was irreversibly surrendering my precious innocent to the outside world.

Hours, often whole days, slip by as I write, looking up from the computer to see that the sun has gone down and my morning coffee, long cold, still waits beside me. I can feel the ache in my core when she disappeared for the first time in a coastal city 2000 miles away and began living on the streets; when I first witnessed her conversing with voices only she could hear; the overwhelming helplessness of trying with my whole being to save her from herself.

I work with boxers of all ages and skill levels. Most of my competitive athletes are in their late teens, twenties, early thirties. I'm their coach, but my relationship feels almost maternal. I care about them and often counsel as much as I coach. While I'm at the gym my traumas and heartaches are put on a shelf, and I focus on my boxers. I'm good at laser-like focus, as though wearing blinders, shining a spotlight on only what I'm choosing to attend to. During my competitive boxing career I could easily direct my adrenaline into the ring, toward the opponent in front of me. Time would slow down, all else would drop away. I have one elite boxer in particular, a woman about my daughter's age. We're close, and it hasn't escaped me that she often receives the attention and emotions that I'd be directing toward Shyloh if she were here.

I often go weeks or months not knowing where Shyloh is, worrying if she's okay, if she's even alive. So I pour myself into my boxers' training, into whatever it is they need from me. It's a balm to have these athletes in my life.

PART ONE

A winter storm blew through last night, sixty-five-plus mile-per-hour gusts toppling vulnerable trees and power lines throughout the area. By sunrise the winds have calmed, and I go out to check the photos of Shyloh hanging from the oak in our yard. This morning most of them lie strewn about the lawn. The few that have held tight are wrapped in tangles among the branches. I have been stubbornly rehanging these pictures since summer, as the summer winds kept taking them down one or two at a time. Each time I retrieve one from the grass, I resist the sharp stabbing sense of loss it brings to see it lying there untethered, and the wave of grief that I know will follow. This morning I gather them up and take them inside, wipe them off and retie the loops. Back outside, as I string them up again and untangle the others from high in the tree, I'm torn by the desperate desire to keep them hanging there, protected forever, and the simultaneous knowledge that it is ultimately, obviously, a futile endeavor. By their very nature, swinging freely in the wind and sun and rain as they are, they will suffer the effects of the elements and eventually, inevitably, degrade. And yet I am compelled to keep repairing and rehanging them, and then once they've been put in order I will sit futilely in the small wooden chair at the edge of the yard with a fleeting sense of something resembling contentment, and watch as her images again dance and twist in the breeze.

BEGINNINGS

Andrea, 3 years old

I was born in Boulder, Colorado. My mom was attending college there, only nineteen years old when she learned she was pregnant. She and my biological father married, but it lasted only a few years, and though he would always send me birthday and Christmas cards, he was mostly absent as I grew up. My mom transferred to the University of Michigan in Ann Arbor, where, when I was a toddler, she met and married my adoptive father, the man I am still proud to call Dad. We lived in Seattle, Washington for several years as he finished his PhD, and when he was offered a professorship at the University of Wisconsin in Madison, we moved and settled there as I was entering the second grade. I've traveled the country as an adult, but strong roots were laid in Wisconsin and to this day, I call Madison home.

Mom worked from home as an editor and freelance writer, and when I was a young child she would play word and writing games with me, teaching me spelling and grammar and a love of books. In my childhood memories, my mother works from bed, writing or reading, two bowls resting next to her on the blankets amidst the notebooks and pencils. One bowl held the sunflower seeds she expertly cracked and separated between her teeth, the other held the hulls. And on the bedside table were nearly always two glasses, one of diet cola, the other Chablis.

I always knew I was loved and she was usually happy when she drank, often singing and hugging me close. But I didn't know how to trust those hugs, I didn't know which version of my mother was holding me. Her moods could fluctuate dramatically, from happy and singing to sobbing behind the locked bathroom door. The inconsistency was confusing and scary. It would be many years before I understood the tenacious grip of alcoholism and depression, of the long family history of mental illness and addiction.

My dad was a professor of cartography and an avid outdoorsman, instilling in me a passion and curiosity for learning and for nature. I don't know what he knew about my mother's drinking and tears; he and I have never discussed it. But he was my rock, giving my early years an emotional predictability that my mother couldn't.

I've been described as a free spirit, wild and rough around the edges. I have always had a love of the physical world, and spent my childhood exploring nature, hunting and gardening with my dad, climbing trees, jumping fences, and almost always barefoot. I'm also an artist at heart, and ever since I could hold a pencil I've been drawing and creating. I've worked in a wide variety of media throughout my life: painting murals, some commissioned, others illicit; tattooing; jewelry making; beading and leatherwork; landscaping. If I see something that catches my eye, I will teach myself to make it.

Though I often railed against authority (still do), I tried to behave (still do). I would get good grades without really trying, absorbing information easily, and if the subject interested me I could focus and work diligently for hours. I have always been bold and adventurous but shy around people. I continue to hold a suspicion of people in general, distrusting others' emotions or intentions. I spent a lot of time playing alone outside as a child, regularly pretending to be a wild animal, a wolf or mountain lion or mustang.

We lived about a mile from the public library, an easy walk on summer afternoons to check out books. *White Fang* and *Call of the Wild* were among my favorites, and science books about animals and Nature, stories of survival in the wilds, of mountain men and Native American crafts. I studied medicinal and edible plants, how to tan hides and make shelters and clothes, how to make and set small animal traps for food, and I would fantasize about living hermit-like in the mountains, scorning all things "civilized" and citified.

But as I entered high school I felt a yearning to fit in, to "belong" to a group. I was far from socially adept; it's not surprising that the circles I gravitated towards in school were on the social fringes too.

And so by age thirteen I was smoking and drinking, and soon skipping class to hang out with the stoners behind the school. I did these things to excess, and would often get black out drunk, wake up and not know where I was or how I got there. It wasn't long before I was chronically truant, I'd get on the public bus in the mornings but instead of getting off at school, I'd stay on and ride it downtown to hang out there with society's outcasts, the vagrants, old hippies, punks, and anarchists. The mental hospitals had recently purged their wards in the spirit of "freedom of choice" and many of these folks wandered the downtown streets too. I left home before my fourteenth birthday to move in with my teenage boyfriend and his free-spirit mother. Social services soon got involved, but even a sixteen-month stint in a juvenile reform school did little more than provide the strict and structured space needed to earn my missed high school credits. This allowed me to graduate, but without ceremony.

I never did move back home. Drawn to the fringes, I favored the rough crowd, and after my release from reform school I went back to live with my boyfriend. It was the mid-1980s, cocaine was everywhere, and he was now a small-time thief and drug dealer. We drank and smoked and began using harder drugs. One night my boyfriend introduced me to the syringe, and I spent the next six months immersed in moderate intravenous drug use. I wish I could explain what miracle saved me from being swept away by it, but my boyfriend was, as were several other friends and acquaintances. I saw what it could do over a relatively short time to an intelligent, functional person, how it could make one sink to previously unthinkable behavior. And from cocaine and crank, I witnessed some move to heroin to help even out their highs. My boyfriend and I ended long nights of partying in drunken muddled arguments; maybe he imagined I'd smiled at another, or he'd misinterpreted a mumbled phrase. Eventually he was blackening my eyes, pummeling my head into the ground in drug-infused furies. He always apologized profusely, professing his eternal love and promising never to do it again, and I stayed with him much longer than I'd like to admit.

He was in jail for assault when I finally moved out and rented my first apartment. I had just turned eighteen. Tracking me down one night soon after his release, he broke in through a window, ripped my phone from the wall and tried to kill me, running off as the police arrived. I was rid of him for good when, to support his ravenous drug habit, he held up a convenience store at gunpoint and was arrested and sentenced to twenty years.

I'd sworn off needles but not the drugs and drinking, and started hanging around biker bars, living a riotous life of parties and motorcycles. I didn't recognize then that I was choosing chaos and adrenaline to mask the internal chaos I was too afraid to acknowledge. I think I felt most comfortable when life was uncomfortable. But I was clearly floundering. I'm stunned I survived.

When I was twenty, I bought an old Ford van and built a bed and cabinets in the back, with a half-baked plan to move into it and travel, maybe west to the mountains or on to California, or maybe north to the Alaskan wilderness, looking for a geographical fix for unacknowledged demons. I informed my landlord I wouldn't be renewing my lease, gave notice at the restaurant where I worked as a cook, closed out my meager bank account, and moved my few possessions into the van.

The eve of my planned departure was spent at the bar drinking and arguing about my plans with Ed, my new boyfriend, and then stumbling to the parking lot at last call to drive drunkenly into the night. Thankfully no one was injured, but the ensuing crash totaled several parked cars as well as my new home.

I was able to get my job at the restaurant back but was scrambling to find somewhere to live, sleeping on couches for the next couple months. It was during this time I discovered I was pregnant.

I think it was not so much a decision as a yielding. I never intended to have children. The emotional and physical responsibility of it terrified me, and I couldn't conceive what it meant to be a mother. But Ed was ecstatic with the prospect of creating a family, and I knew that I desperately needed to change course from what I'd been doing. So, we moved in together and set up house.

I was told by those close to me that being pregnant "softened my edges." My rebellious and reckless lifestyle was now tempered with uncharacteristic caution. I stopped drinking and using drugs while I was pregnant and started imagining a different life.

SHYLOH – MAY 12, 1988

Shyloh, 1 year old

I'd fallen in love with Shyloh as she kicked and somersaulted in my belly, but when I first looked into her small face I was overwhelmed by the intensity and power of that love, by the maternal realization that I wouldn't hesitate to give my life for her. And I know without question that loving her saved my life.

Even as a baby Shyloh could light up a room with her beautiful, contagious laugh, open mouthed and open hearted, golden green eyes twinkling. As soon as she could walk she toddled easily up to strangers to enchant them with babbling conversations and laughter. And through the years, nearly all who ever met my daughter were drawn magnetically to her, one of those generous spirits who would make friends with anyone, who would make you feel as though you were the center of her world. Unlike me, she seemed to thrive on being around people and had the ability to slide seamlessly between vastly diverse social circles. But like me, in her teens she gravitated towards the fringes, towards the darker side of life. And, like the large, intricate chameleon she would one day have tattooed on her forearm, her ability to easily transform herself to fit her surroundings would also become apparent.

She had dark moments too, that were equally potent. Her first year of life she would wake during the night and scream inconsolably for hours. I tried everything I could think of, holding her close and rocking her, pacing the floor with her, singing to her. Sometimes I would eventually have to just shut her door, covering my ears from the other room and cry along with her. It tore at my heart to not be able to offer any comfort to whatever was torturing her. She finally grew out of those night terrors, but her demons would reappear in her early teens. She would find alcohol, then harder drugs, and I know she used these to temporarily fill that dark place inside. I know because I'd done it for years myself.

Shyloh was about a year old when Ed started staying out all night, sometimes all weekend, especially after payday. I was working as a cook, a freelance artist and tattooist at the time, and he as an apprentice carpenter. When the pool cue he'd bought me for my birthday disappeared, I realized he was selling our things to buy drugs. I eventually took Shyloh and moved out. Ed made a dramatic reversal from drugs and alcohol to the Pentecostal Church, but when he understood we weren't coming back, he left for San Diego and out of our lives.

Shyloh's adoptive father, the man who would become my husband for the next twenty years, was sober when we started dating, though he too had a long history of alcohol and drug abuse. Marc had retired early from the Army Infantry due to a serious injury, but he held to a strong sense of duty and honor that had been instilled in him there. I think I'd mistaken these qualities along with his sobriety for maturity, and believed I had found

stability and true love for myself and my daughter. He had a temper, would sometimes upend the kitchen table, sometimes throw and break things, but he never hit me and I was comfortable living with emotional unease and turbulence. Shyloh and I moved in with him, Marc and I married soon after, and three and a half years later Shyloh's brother, Zeke, was born.

Shyloh and baby Zeke

Marc and I sold our motorcycles and settled on a gorgeous piece of land in the driftless area in southwest Wisconsin, forty-plus acres of hardwoods and sandstone cliffs and meadows. I studied the native flora and excitedly discovered remnant oak savannas and short grass prairies. We gardened, hunted, raised chickens, picked wild berries, and took long walks in the woods. And when the kids and I weren't outdoors, we were often inside at the kitchen table reading or doing crafts. I loved teaching them both how to make things, and Shyloh especially enjoyed crafting with me.

I took Shyloh with me one afternoon to shop for light fixtures, giving her the task of choosing a new one for her bedroom. Wide-eyed and beaming with excitement, she pointed immediately to the lavish chandelier dripping with glittering crystals that hung above us, something meant to adorn a grand ballroom and not an eight-year old's bedroom. I laughed and explained that she could have a chandelier once she was grown and had her own house. Her response, serious and with typical Shyloh-logic, "But then I'll have too much sense to get a chandelier!"

My husband first got me into martial arts. I am by nature obsessive and driven and would train for hours each day, compelled by a desire for perfection. After a relatively short time I earned my first and then second degree black belt in Okinawan Shorin Ryu, and a first degree in Okinawan weaponry. And then when I needed a new challenge, Marc found the boxing coach who would later become my manager, men-

tor, and good friend. It was the mid-1990s and women's boxing was only beginning to become a thing. I would spar with
the men in the gym but struggled to find female opponents
for competition as an amateur boxer. I took several semi-pro
kickboxing matches and entered a Toughman tournament just
to get ring time before turning pro at thirty-three years old.

I loved boxing – the challenge, the intense training, the
adrenaline. I was a natural athlete with a strong aggressive
personality honed by a life of defiance. It was clear to me too
that the exercise and training had taken the place of drugs
and alcohol. I would take the kids with me to the gym while
I sparred, Shyloh dutifully doing her homework or reading a
book, Zeke fidgeting and restless. They would follow along
on their bikes while I ran trails for conditioning and would
wait impatiently for me to come upstairs from my incessant
heavy bag workouts in the basement. And they would often
climb through the ropes to hop excitedly in the ring as my
hand was raised after a win. And I won often.

I remember during an after-fight interview, the incredulous look the reporter gave me when I replied that no, it
didn't really hurt that much getting punched in the face. But
it didn't. Getting punched in the face can be jarring, make
your eyes water, bloody your nose and blacken your eyes,
but when you're trained to see punches coming your hands
are up and ready to block, your feet are balanced under you
so you can move your head and let the punches slip by, and
when one does connect, you've learned to roll with it to reduce its impact. Maybe I simply knew what it felt like, so it

didn't scare me. Maybe now that I was trained to face the attacks head on, the physical pain was secondary. A gut punch though, that's different. A gut punch attacks your core. All you can do is contract your conditioned abs to mute the blow, assuming you've seen it coming. With a powerful snapping punch to the liver, the right side just under the ribs, there's a few second delay when you know you've been hit, and then the bile green wave of nausea. Strength and will have nothing to do with it. It will drop you to your knees. I've never been dropped in the ring by one myself, but I've dropped others. I've seen that look.

In fact, I was never really hurt during competition; my aggressive offense generally pushed right past anything my opponents tried to throw at me. I did experience a few injuries from sparring, though: a broken nose from an errant elbow, a dislocated jaw when a right hook caught me with my hands down, and had my front teeth replaced after the roots were cracked from an unexpected head-butt. I was knocked out only once during the years I boxed, for just a couple seconds when I was training for a kickboxing match and the guy I was sparring caught me with a roundhouse kick to the side of the head. The next thing I knew I was getting back up from the canvas, a little disoriented, a bit of a headache later that night. I suffered way more concussions and black eyes from my teenage boyfriend. Winning never fueled me, it was about controlling my opponent, controlling the fight. I confronted core demons every time I climbed between those ropes and that was making me stronger, more confident.

I pushed myself nonstop for years, trained relentlessly, and took ibuprofen, as much as 3200mg for days in a row to push through the overtraining injuries that were beginning to physically break me down. After another year of training through pain, I knew competition at this level was no longer sustainable. I needed multiple surgeries: on my elbow to remove bone chips from hitting the heavy bag too much; knee surgery to clean up a torn meniscus from the ceaseless road running; hip surgery to remove bone spurs and torn cartilage. I also had chronic low back pain. I felt an immense loss when after eleven professional fights, I made the difficult decision to retire. But I knew in my bones I could carry that confidence gained in the ring on to the rest of my life. I believed I could do anything I set my mind to.

A deep void was left in me when I stopped competing. Finding solace in forging a deeper connection with our land, I prepared to convert a fallow ten-acre cornfield into prairie grasses and flowers. While shopping for seed at a nearby prairie nursery, I casually inquired about a job and started work as a laborer the next day. My initial tasks were collecting and cleaning seed, digging plants for bare root sales, and weeding, but within a year I became the nursery manager, overseeing seed and plant orders, and leading offsite crews to do prairie installations and prescribed burns. The work was quite literally restorative for both the land and me, being outdoors all day, hands in the dirt and usually barefoot, surrounded by native flowers and grasses and fresh air.

While I was busy planting prairies, Shyloh was beginning to navigate adolescence. At times her moods would swing wildly, and her behavior could be quite impulsive. But everyone knows teenagers are "nuts" and compared to my own experiences as a teen, I believed our family was weathering the relative chaos well.

Once, though, she went so far as to make a "suicidal gesture" by scratching at her wrists and was taken into protective custody for seventy-two hours in Boscobel Area Healthcare's mental health unit (the hospital's mental health unit closed a few years later due to lack of funding). She was fourteen. Doctors put her on antidepressants, but when the medication made her moods and behavior even more erratic, we tossed them, just as the evening news began reporting that Prozac could have serious side effects when given to young people. At the time my husband and I had a general distrust of "big Pharma" and this news reinforced these beliefs. Shyloh received a few months of counseling and quickly charmed her therapist. I don't believe she was consciously lying or manipulative, though she may have been; she literally charmed everyone, including her therapist. Her energy was magnetic.

Though not especially athletic as a child, Shyloh courageously tried everything at least once; in seventh grade she even joined the boys wrestling team. I was supportive but would grimace while watching her practices. She was clearly way over her head, the only girl on the team, and a complete novice against boys who'd been doing it since kindergarten. Even so, she pushed through these training sessions, and valiantly walked out on the mat for her first and only competition to get pinned almost immediately. She expressed only mild disappointment, brushed herself off, and moved on to something new, and I couldn't help but be impressed by her impossible confidence. She consistently made the honor roll throughout middle and high school and excelled in creative writing and art. And though she loved to read, often spending hours in her room with her face buried in a book, she was a people person, relishing being part of any group. Choir was one of her favorites, her voice strong and soulful, and in high school she was even awarded scholarships several years in a row to attend a summer choir camp at a nearby university campus, which she attended with enthusiasm. She joined speech and debate and theater, and played one season each of most of the sports the small high school offered to girls: volleyball, basketball, gymnastics, cheerleading.

I had never played team sports or joined any clubs, hadn't had anything close to a normal high school experience. My heart swelled as she explored things I'd never done. I admired her courage and effortless ability to connect with people, to compel others to open their hearts to her, how generously she could give of herself, qualities I've never felt able to express without great effort. I imagined her adolescence would be "normal," that she would show me what it was supposed to look like.

But familiarity often allows dysfunction to feel normal, jarring as it may be. And so it was when her dad and I discovered she was also drinking and getting high. Concerned friends would call me late at night to confide where they were partying so I could come get her, warning that she was passed out or blackout drunk. Our suspicion that she was involved with harder drugs was confirmed when the school called to inform us she'd been arrested for cocaine possession with intent to deliver. I believed I was leading by example; my husband and I had both quit smoking and drinking years ago, we didn't do drugs anymore and spoke strongly against them, ate healthily and exercised. I felt such helplessness watching her follow in a path I hadn't even known I'd left for her.

We found her a lawyer, the friend of a neighbor, and the charges were ultimately dropped with Shyloh agreeing to get counseling for alcohol and drug abuse. And as if to highlight her ability to charm, that lawyer went on to hire Shyloh to work in the law office answering phones and doing odd jobs over the summer and through her senior year. Our family began what would become years of counseling. Witnessing my daughter's teen struggles forced me to confront traumas from my own adolescence, long since buried, and I began seeing my own counselor. I read interpretations of the *Tao Te Ching* and other books on Taoism, feeling a strong connection to the sentiment of Oneness and of letting go. We had again weathered the storm.

Shyloh excelled in counseling, if such a thing can be said. She soon became a mentor for others who were struggling with drugs and alcohol, helped run group sessions, and even started working with a wilderness program for troubled teens. I watched with tears of pride as she stepped onto the stage in cap and gown to receive her high school diploma. She would be heading to the University of Wisconsin, Platteville in the fall, double majoring in psychology and criminal justice and I was quietly amazed at how fluidly she seemed to have navigated through all of it.

I had been working at the prairie nursery for about six years when the owner informed me she was selling the business. The new owners asked me to stay on in my same role, and I worked with them for a season, but most of my coworkers had left already and it felt like a good time for me to move on too. I began exploring other opportunities.

Shyloh's classes would start soon and she had just moved into her dorm room in Platteville. Zeke was consumed with middle school football and learning everything there was to know about muscle cars. With my husband's encouragement and support, I considered going back to school, something I'd never before imagined. This felt like the right time. Shyloh and I shopped together for laptops, notebooks and binders, and giggled at the idea of mother and daughter attending college at the same time.

I'd been treated for lots of training injuries throughout my boxing career and viewed physical therapy as a kind of magic, so I decided to pursue a degree in Sports Medicine. I had a lot of catching up to do, though, having graduated high school with only the barest minimum of credits. After a very intense year and a half at a community college to make up the credits necessary to enter a large university, I applied and was accepted into University of Wisconsin, Madison's Kinesiology program, with a goal of working in physical rehab and specializing with athletes.

I surprised myself by how much I enjoyed school as an adult, relishing the new challenges, and as with everything else I committed to, threw myself in with both feet. When I wasn't studying or driving Zeke to and from football practices, I was doing landscape consulting and native plant gardening, having started my own small business. Working outside with the flowers and grasses kept me grounded, and I was good at it. I didn't advertise but clients sought me out anyway; it made sense to get paid for something I loved to do. And, I needed to stay constantly occupied. I put tremendous effort into distracting myself from the storm of emotions that still threatened to swallow me.

Around this time my former boxing coach/manager invited me to help him supervise sparring and teach boxing classes at the gym twice a week. I'd missed boxing, and even though I would be on the other side of the ropes, I was thrilled to be involved in the sport again. I reveled in being so busy, in the variety each day held, and in falling exhausted into bed each night.

I was straightening up Shyloh's room one afternoon after she moved into her college dorm that fall. Her bedroom walls still displayed the colorful life-sized butterflies I had painted on them years earlier. I thought back to when Shyloh was four years old and wanted to be a butterfly for Halloween. We made the costume together, her fabric wings attached at the wrists and the large iridescent spots sparkling as her butterfly arms waved, fuzzy pipe cleaner antennae tipped with cotton-balls bobbing on top of her head. With glittery face paint we created large butterfly eyes, and she fluttered and twirled around the living room all morning, face beaming with the carefree spirit of a swallowtail. Her preschool class had a costume party that afternoon. When we arrived and she saw another little girl with a butterfly costume, Shyloh ran straight to her with smile and wings wide as she said, "Let's go fly!"

The painted butterflies on her walls flitted amongst the many photos she'd tacked here and there, of birthdays and holidays with family, and years of adventures with her many friends. Multiple bookshelves, stored with the volumes she loved to reread, were adorned with collections and personal treasures gathered over the years. I smiled as I pulled out boxes from her closet. The first couple were crammed full of selected schoolwork from as far back as elementary school, penmanship assignments, book reports, report cards, honor roll certificates, art projects. In another box, a childhood's worth of letters from relatives and friends, diaries and poems and sketches, every birthday card and Valentine I'd ever made for her. I would tease her lovingly about this habit of hers to save everything, and she would laugh at herself unselfconsciously. But I understood.

You find security in holding tightly to relics like these, as if without them, in losing sight of who you were, you might forget who you are.

When years later she began to leave everything behind, little by little, long-valued possessions, then friends, and then family, the letting go of all she held dear was all the more striking by contrast.

Shyloh's first solo bike ride

HEROIN – 2006

Platteville, Wisconsin was a mere half hour drive from home and Shyloh would visit nearly every weekend that first year, excitedly sharing with us her "adulting" adventures as she referred to them. Eager to have her own space her second year, she convinced us to let her move from the dorms to an apartment off-campus. She called and visited less often then, but the winds were calm. I felt such relief believing she had found her way. She was in college and had a part-time job, was dating a smart, charming boyfriend she adored, who adored her too. The whole world seemed to lie at her feet. When the used car we'd given her to travel back and forth from college was totaled, she explained she hadn't been driving, that a friend had borrowed it. We helped her get another, and when unpaid parking tickets and then impound notices started showing up in the mail, she easily explained these away as well, and I must have willingly stayed ignorant. I desperately wanted to believe what I was seeing on the surface. I had developed a hyper-vigilance, probably since childhood, always scanning faces to detect the truths behind the words, prepared for whatever looming danger might be lurking. But, that hyper-vigilance can fail when the need for blinders arises in order to keep moving forward. I wore blinders to block out the chaos and uncertainty. I kept moving forward.

The summer before Shyloh's junior year in college, Marc and I received a call from a police officer with the news that our daughter had overdosed on heroin. We were thrown into a shocked panic. I knew she went out partying with friends, but heroin was not even on our radar. The officer informed us that EMS had revived her and she was in stable condition but would be going to jail. It was 2008, and it wouldn't be until 2013 that the Good Samaritan law would be passed, granting immunity from prosecution for people requiring treatment for an overdose. And so, after being revived and stabilized, Shyloh was charged with criminal possession, given four months in jail and put on a waitlist for a spot at a residential drug and alcohol treatment facility as a required condition of her release. She tearfully sobbed apologies, and emphatically swore for positive changes. She and I wrote letters back and forth and talked on the phone nearly daily while she waited out her sentence. I sent her the books on meditation and self-help she requested, and she delved in, determined to disentangle negative patterns of behavior. I was amazed at how well she had kept hidden the drug use and whatever else haunted her, but she confessed to me that she was tired of lying and pretending. I was hopeful again that we were finding our way back to a path of healing and recovery.

I suspect it was her beloved college boyfriend who called EMS that night, as we later learned they'd been using together for months. With cruel irony, Shyloh would begin her ninety-day treatment program the same day we received the call that he'd been found dead in his bedroom from an opioid overdose. She rarely mentioned him again except when the calendar would near the anniversary of his death, but I knew she was tormented with guilt and shame that he had died and she had lived.

Deciding to take more time off from school, Shyloh was again deeply involved with counseling and mentoring and helping to guide struggling teens on wilderness expeditions. Being on these treks, surrounded by nature and the incredible vistas they encountered, was something she later wrote about for a journaling exercise as one of her two most memorable experiences. While on a winter trek, she tore a ligament in her knee when her leg unexpectedly broke through deep snow and torqued the joint. She was devastated when she believed she would be giving up the trails indefinitely.

For Shyloh's twenty-first birthday, I arranged a skydiving lesson as a surprise and she would later write about this as her second most memorable experience. A born adrenaline seeker, she remembered vividly the feeling of "... jumping from a perfectly good airplane to fall weightless through the air, a moment frozen in time, celebrating sobriety, loving life." I think she craved that feeling of completely letting go of all that tethered her to earth, freedom from all expectation and responsibility and potential. I imagine that's what the drugs did for her too.

Then at fifteen, Shyloh's brother began struggling with drugs and alcohol too. We again delved into family counseling but ultimately our family was too fractured, and the stress of confronting our individual pasts proved too much. My husband packed his bags one day and left, and Zeke, angry and confused, went with him. In an agonizing coincidence, Shyloh had moved back home the same day and I saw the fresh needle marks on her arms. She stayed close to me that first week and we held each other for hours as we both cried, heartbroken by the ruins of our small family, by the compounding sorrows of both our lives. But ultimately I told Shyloh she would have to choose between the drugs and staying. She chose the drugs.

This period marked one of the deepest lows in my life. Serious thoughts of suicide consumed me for months. Each day I would get up and go through the motions of living, of going to school, now only one year from my degree, and then to the gym to coach and teach classes. On the weekends, I would do my landscaping work. I was getting good at compartmentalizing grief and trauma; one day at a time, one foot in front of the other.

Shyloh and I talked on the phone often. She lost a few more good friends to either suicide or overdose and became newly committed to recovery, again. She promised to be completely honest with me from then on. She wasn't going to lie about her drug use anymore, not necessarily promising never to use again, but acknowledging the need to take full responsibility for her choices and actions. She had a verse of the serenity prayer tattooed on her upper arm, opposite the large sunflower covering her other shoulder.

> *God grant me the serenity*
> *To accept the things I cannot change;*
> *Courage to change the things I can;*
> *And wisdom to know the difference.*

My mother had also gone through changes. With the help of antidepressants she was finally pulled out of years-long depression. She stopped drinking around the time Shyloh was born, having done the hard emotional work of self-discovery, and was working on a book (that she would later self-publish as *Waking Up Happy)* about what comes after. Each chapter was a personal account of addiction and recovery, her own and others, and the various tools used by each to heal. Shyloh and I both added our own chapters and it again felt as though the storms had passed.

JAMES – 2011

I met James at the gym at the end of that year. We started dating after a few months and I could imagine living again. This relationship was vastly different than others I'd had. He was kind and emotionally mature, practical and responsible, intelligent and funny. He had never used drugs or abused alcohol and had a quiet but extraordinary strength that didn't require constant validation. After dating for three years we moved in together into a house on a 1.3 acre lot surrounded by gorgeous mature oaks, and it felt implausibly secluded even though we were in the middle of town. We raised chickens and bees, grew fruit trees and vegetable gardens. I planted prairie flowers and berry patches and built a 1200-square foot outbuilding at the edge of the property that we used as a gym.

My son had put up a nearly impenetrable emotional wall and our relationship remained strained after the divorce, but both he and Shyloh would stay with James and me off and on over the next couple years while they each struggled to find their way. Having abruptly lost the shared place that held our memories, my children and I felt tossed into the wind. But as

I was ready to again try setting down roots, Shyloh was letting each powerful gust take her further and further from the stable life I hoped for her. In her own words, she was "being drawn to the dark side."

Shyloh had just broken up with her new boyfriend when she confessed to me they'd been smoking crack. Though thankful she was confiding in me, my heart sank with disappointment. A couple weeks had gone by without hearing from her when I received a message from her ex that he knew where she was. He was really worried about her. The new guy she was with was a dealer, crack and heroin, and Shyloh was in deep. He gave me the address, a middle-class house in a residential neighborhood, up the block from the gym where I coached boxing.

The windows were covered with dark paper from the inside, the large wooden doors deadbolted; one of the small windows in back had been boarded over. I pounded on the doors, front and back, yelling her name loudly for several minutes until finally she opened the back door and came out. She looked terrible, gaunt, in baggy sweatpants and a dark hoodie. She had the yellowy, green remnants of a black eye and her hair was in unwashed tangles around her face. Twitchy and agitated, she was more than a little amazed I was there, demanding to know how I'd found her. I didn't say. I begged her to come with me over and over but she refused, finally saying she had to go. I grabbed and hugged her tight to my chest, told her I loved her. "I love you too, Mama," she said, then turned and went back inside.

I immediately called the police and was told, as I would be told over and over in the years to come, that because my daughter was an adult, her choices were her own. I was told that without witnessing money and drugs exchange hands, they would do nothing. I hung up furious and ready for battle.

I went home and started making calls, forging a plan for how to get Shyloh out of there and what to do with her once I did. James helped by searching property listings online, and was able to track down the name and number of the woman who owned the house. I called and told the woman what I knew, that her property was being used as a drug house and that my daughter was there, a subtle threat implied in my tone. I heard the defensiveness in the woman's voice turn to frustration and then resignation, as she confessed finally that it was her son who lived there, that he'd sworn to her months ago he was done with "that stuff." She agreed to meet me at the house with a key.

My blood was coursing with adrenaline as the woman unlocked the front door. I had no idea what to expect when I walked in, but the put-together exterior of the house was irreconcilable with the filth and disorder of the interior. I had a singular focus and only vaguely recall the garbage and several bodies lying huddled under blankets and jackets around the living room floor. I moved determinedly through the lower level looking in every corner and demanding from anyone who seemed conscious to tell me where Shyloh was. Someone said upstairs in a bedroom.

I clearly remember pushing open that bedroom door and

seeing her lying there, skeletally thin, barely dressed, curled up on the filthy floor. Needles lay scattered around her on the carpet, some new, some used; a partially eaten bowl of plain pasta lay near her head. Her scalp was shaven. An electric razor lay nearby amid clumps of her hair. I could hear chaos in the hallway. I suspect it was the mother confronting her son, but their troubles didn't interest me. It wasn't easy to rouse Shyloh, and when she woke she was confused and belligerent. I told her she was coming home with me, and she argued weakly at first, then sobbed and let me wrap a blanket around her and sat as I gathered up her few belongings.

Shyloh had fallen to what we all believed must be "the bottom" and she courageously pulled herself out of those depths, valiantly paving yet another new path.

But she would repeat this cycle over and over, falling a little deeper each time, clearly bottomless. It was both exhausting and heartbreaking to witness, but I stubbornly stayed by her side through each stumble, each fall, each climb. She would dive back into the twelve steps of AA and NA (narcotics anonymous). If I didn't hear from her for several days in a row I'd start to worry, suspecting she'd relapsed again, and then after a month or two we'd start the process over. I began to think the words "relapse" and "recovery" and "bottom" were meaningless, that there was no true recovery; the addiction alone would change. And that the only true bottom was death. Addiction is so complicated and often tightly woven together with other mental illnesses. It's often not the physical yearning that's so hard to manage, but the emotional void that needs to be filled, the overactive circuitry that needs to be muted, the missing brain chemicals that the addict is unconsciously striving to replace. We hear of people who can quit and walk away. I was somehow able to walk away from the drugs, but for years I filled that void with other extreme behaviors. Exercise is obviously good for you; using it as I did probably wasn't. But I also won't likely lose my job or my home or my friends and family from my overtraining. I won't likely die from it.

Shyloh was physically gorgeous by most standards, probably could've been a model, even with the gauged ears and all her tattoos. She could transform her appearance on a whim and often did, one day a platinum blonde and buxom with the help of padded pushup bras, fully adorned with painted nails, makeup and six-inch stiletto heels. Then she'd be a hip skater chick or a tattooed gangster, a rugged outdoorsy woman or the "girl next door." And she did these transformations so effortlessly that it was more a marvel than jarring. She worked for a while in a tattoo shop doing piercings and sold hemp crafts on Etsy, with the online tag "Shy Knot Shy," a play on words for the knotted macrame necklaces she made and, I suspect in retrospect, also hinting towards still mostly closeted struggles with an emerging mental illness. She was able to find work easily, getting hired for nearly every job she applied for, though she never seemed to set her sights very high and would bounce from job to job: store clerk, cashier, waitress, barista. She did the same with boyfriends, gravitating now towards troubled men with a desire to save them. She would fall hard, even planned a few weddings, but all ultimately unraveled within a year. Each time she would start over, the new apartment would be thoughtfully decorated with the secondhand treasures we'd find discarded curbside or shopping at St. Vincent's, and we'd talk or text nearly every day.

At one point Shyloh needed a psychological evaluation as a requirement to get a bed at an inpatient rehab. She was given a tentative diagnosis of *borderline personality disorder* and/or *bipolar disorder*, with co-occurring substance use which we all agreed was likely a form of self-medication.

Diagnosing mental illness is complicated, as everything lies on a spectrum, but it is known to be heritable and we began to outline a family history of mental illness going back several generations on both sides of her family tree: paranoid schizophrenia, bipolar disorder, depression, severe anxiety, obsessive compulsive disorder, oppositional defiance disorder, each with associated addictions. I became very familiar with the DSM – the Diagnostic and Statistical Manual of Mental Disorders. If you google "borderline personality disorder" or "bipolar disorder," you will likely find some variation of the following (modified from whatever the current wording is in the DSM at the time you are searching):

> ***Borderline Personality Disorder*** *– involves a longstanding pattern of abrupt, moment-to-moment swings — in moods, relationships, self-image, and behavior (in contrast to distinct episodes of mania or depression in people with bipolar disorder) that*

are usually triggered by conflicts in interactions with other people. DSM definition: a pervasive pattern of instability in interpersonal relationships, self-image, and emotion, as well as marked impulsivity beginning by early adulthood and present in a variety of contexts, as indicated by five (or more) of the following: chronic feelings of emptiness; emotional instability in reaction to day-to-day events (e.g., intense episodic sadness, irritability, or anxiety usually lasting a few hours and only rarely more than a few days); frantic efforts to avoid real or imagined abandonment; identity disturbance with markedly or persistently unstable self-image or sense of self; impulsive behavior in at least two areas that are potentially self-damaging (e.g., spending, sex, substance abuse, reckless driving, binge eating); inappropriate, intense anger or difficulty controlling anger (e.g., frequent displays of temper, constant anger, recurrent physical fights); pattern of unstable and intense interpersonal relationships characterized by extremes between idealization and devaluation (also known as "splitting"); recurrent suicidal behavior, gestures, or threats, or self-harming behavior; transient, stress-related paranoid ideation or severe dissociative symptoms.

Bipolar Disorder – a disorder associated with episodes of mood swings ranging from depressive lows to manic highs. The exact cause of bipolar disorder

*isn't known, but a combination of genetics, environ-
ment, and altered brain structure and chemistry may
play a role. Manic episodes may include symptoms
such as high energy, reduced need for sleep, and loss
of touch with reality. Depressive episodes may include
symptoms such as low energy, low motivation, and
loss of interest in daily activities. Mood episodes last
days to months at a time and may also be associated
with suicidal thoughts. Treatment is usually lifelong
and often involves a combination of medications and
psychotherapy.*

Shyloh was prescribed various medications over the
next several years: lamotrigine, a mood stabilizer; loraz-
epam, an anti-anxiety med; risperidone, an antipsychotic,
and was again going to counseling regularly. She had by
now mastered the process if not the results, journaling diligently, pouring over self-help workbooks, and together she
and I learned about Cognitive Behavioral Therapy (CBT)
and Dialectic Behavioral Therapy (DBT) and, from my van-
tage point anyway, the medications seemed to ease the gusts
that kept blowing her off course. But to work well they have
to be taken consistently.

GEOGRAPHICAL FIX - 2016

I finished my Bachelor's degree and became licensed as an athletic trainer. Athletic training usually brings up images of personal fitness trainers when in actuality we are healthcare workers and our expertise lies in recognizing, preventing and rehabilitating musculoskeletal injuries. We are often the first responders for injury during sporting events, and I was hired soon after graduation to do outreach for a local hospital covering high school sports, most often football, wrestling and hockey. I especially enjoyed the "detective" aspect of determining the cause of an injury and putting together a rehabilitation plan.

Around this same time, after more than sixty years in the sport, my former boxing coach was ready to step away and hand me the reins to take over the entire amateur boxing program at the gym. I had been helping him for just over a decade by then, having already coached several successful competitive boxers of my own. I accepted the challenge with honor and pride. Four days each week I was at the gym giving personal boxing lessons, supervising sparring, and teaching the classes. I also started a special boxing program for people with Parkinson's.

I threw myself into these activities, and into my own physical training: running, weightlifting, boxing, and the distractions kept me grounded. Exercise had become my drug and escape years ago, and I often utilized my newly acquired knowledge to rehabilitate my own training injuries as well as those of my boxers.

Shyloh and her latest boyfriend, Matt, had recently had a violent breakup, he'd moved out, and she was inconsolable. Searching for something to hold on to, she ambitiously applied for and received an informational packet to start her own Narcotics Anonymous chapter in her neighborhood. It would take several months of red tape to get it going, so she decided that in the interim a change of scenery would help get her head straight.

Shyloh had met Ed, her biological father, only once since he left when she was a baby, when at eighteen she reached out to him and asked if she could come for a visit. I remember going through something similar in my teens, imagining that the absent biological parent I'd placed on a pedestal my entire childhood held The Key, only to find him to be self-indulgent and imperfect in real life. But at twenty-eight, Shyloh was convinced that Ed's love and acceptance were the missing pieces to her wellbeing and she reached out to him again. I was skeptical, but reluctant to stand in the way of self-discovery and potential healing. I did try to discourage her new grand plan, though, to fly out to San Diego and stay with Ed and his family for a couple months. Ed readily agreed, offering to let her stay with him and his wife and twin daughters,

Shyloh's half-sisters. He even had a job for her helping to manage one of his low-income apartment buildings so she could build up a little savings. In early December of 2016, I dropped Shyloh off at the airport and we held each other in a tight embrace, promising that we would write and call each other often, that she'd be back in a few months.

SAN DIEGO – 2017

Many of the tenants in Ed's apartment complexes strug-gled with mental illness and were coming from homeless situations. Shyloh was so excited with her new responsibili-ties, to prepare and serve three meals per day for the resi-dents, and to dispense their meds – technically not legal but a needed service. We wrote letters weekly, but she would often call me several times a day and text pictures of San Diego's amazing flora and of the creative meals she was teaching herself to make.

> "Greetings from Cali!... So one of the worst things about living here?? THE BUGS! Cockroaches dude... it's apparently a big problem in southern states. They don't sting or bite & they run away when you get near but they're EVERYWHERE! This rant is brought to you by the inch long roach that was peering over my shoulder at this letter. BLEGH! If you don't believe me, I promise I'll squish one & mail it home to you. hahaha

Here's my fav part of this book Gma sent me, called Love Warrior: "What I want to be isn't sexy or pretty as much as beautiful. Beautiful means full of beauty. Beautiful is not about how you look on the outside, Beautiful is about what you're made of. Beautiful people spend time discovering what their idea of beauty on this earth is. They know themselves well enough to know what they love, and they know themselves well enough to fill up with a little bit of their particular kind of beauty each day." Love that. Also from that book: AFGO – Another Fucking Growth Opportunity ... clever lil acronym ehh?"

Shyloh expressed concern that her own meds were running low and because she didn't have another prescription for refills, and didn't have insurance to find someone who'd write her a new one, we discussed the idea of weaning off of them while she was in California. She was optimistic that she didn't need them anymore, and honestly I was hopeful too. Her dosages were relatively low but I knew that stopping antipsychotics or mood stabilizers abruptly could be dangerous. So after extensive research online, I helped her lay out a schedule for slowly lowering her doses based on how much she had left with careful monitoring, with a ridiculously vague plan that if she started noticing any serious side effects she would contact a mental health worker for professional guidance. We stayed in close contact during this time and she would relay to me, sometimes hourly, how she was feeling as the doses were gradually decreased, and then finally gone. At first she would describe to me the slightest differences she was noticing in mood, and then I began noticing a manic energy to her speech and writing. Something was clearly off, but was it just being off her meds or was she using again? Her creative meals started getting stranger. We spoke several times a week, but when I expressed my concerns she would assure me she felt GREAT, that everything was AMAZING. She wasn't calling and writing as often and had reverted to texting me pictures, emojis and short perky messages instead of picking up the phone when I'd call.

Shyloh and her ex, Matt, started corresponding again. I'd been expecting her to move back home in the spring, but instead she met up with Matt, and in impulsive-Shyloh-fashion they flew to Vegas and got married, then back to San Diego to set up house. For a month or so she and I again talked regularly. She was excited and a little nervous about her new role as "wife" and reached out to me as a newly married daughter to her mother for advice on issues big and small.

Matt and Shyloh had always been good friends and cared deeply for each other, but their relationship was troubled before and it clearly was still. The marriage lasted only a few months before imploding. Matt abruptly left for Denver to stay with friends, leaving Shyloh behind, again devastated. She stopped answering my calls. Then Ed told me she wasn't keeping up with her apartment management responsibilities, that she was selling her things, first the sewing machine I'd bought her as a wedding gift, then her bike, then everything else. When confronted, Matt confessed that towards the end of their time together he and Shyloh were smoking crack again.

Shyloh tearfully agreed to two weeks in Detox after Ed threatened to kick her out of her apartment, and from Detox, a bed waited for her at a ninety-day treatment program. She was committed to saving her marriage, she said, and hoped that she and Matt could still make a life together in San Diego.

She finished her two-week detox but never showed up to the treatment center. After hearing nothing from her for several days I called the detox facility to inquire, but because of privacy laws they wouldn't confirm that she'd even been there. The police were able to get the information I couldn't, confirming that she had indeed been released from Detox on the date

I'd given them. With rising panic, I filed an official missing person's report, and then waited.

Shyloh, San Diego

PART TWO

I'm haunted by the horrors I imagine have taken her, and I'm newly obsessed with an idea of flying to San Diego to find her. But I'm absolutely daunted with how to even start searching in a city of that size, totally foreign to me, knowing nothing about where she goes, who she knows, a precious grain of sand lost on a beach 2000 miles away.

Weeks go by and I hear nothing. I check in with the San Diego police every few days, and I distract myself at the gym, putting my energy into my boxers. I have several elite fighters that I'll be taking to national tournaments this year, and I'm able to temporarily put aside the ache in my chest while I focus on their dreams.

Two long months go by with no word, until I get a call one morning from an unknown number, a California area code. "Hi, Mama."

FIRST VISIT – DECEMBER 2017

It's been six weeks since that call, and just over a year since Shyloh and I hugged goodbye at the airport in Madison. I'm impatient to see her. James and I finally land in San Diego, the first time here for both of us, and we're heading to the address Shyloh gave me. It's not her place but a friend of a friend's, her new boyfriend, Tyler, and his benefactor, Bill. She tells me she wants to be sure to have showered, to have an address for us to meet her.

"I don't want you to have to see firsthand how I've been living these past several months haha! :)- " she messages, and I'm grateful for this small mercy.

She has no phone but has been staying in touch with me via Facebook lately. I generally loathe Facebook, but recently downloaded the Messenger app on my phone for this purpose. San Diego's downtown public library has computers she can use and through Facebook Messenger she fills me in, explains how she "discovered" meth while in Detox, how she truly meant to go to the rehab center when released but, someone offered and she couldn't resist, how the past several months have been a drug-infused adventure. She confides that she really is trying to quit the drugs but confesses frankly that she enjoys the challenge of this untethered life.

"The struggle is legit real, Mama, but I'm learning the tricks!" I hear a modest pride in her voice. My mother-bear self wants to snatch her up and drag her home where I can keep her safe and talk sense into her. But there's another long-ago part of me that gets it, that appreciates the allure of narrowing life down to its absolute basics, and I feel the absurdity of these two realities trying to live together inside my head.

Ed still has the clothes and a few other things Shyloh left behind in the apartment, and has been taking care of Rocco, the little white chihuahua she and Matt adopted when they first set up house. James and I arrange to pick up her things, and there's a conversation about the dog and if we could take him too, if Shyloh is capable right now of taking care of him. We decide to wait on the dog.

She's jittery but pleasant and we fall into our comfortable way of talking and giggling. She stays with us at our airbnb and I can hear her up all night arranging and rearranging the suitcases full of clothes. Some of her things she asks me to take back with us for safe keeping, a quilt I'd made for her when she'd left for college years ago, a pair of porcupine earrings and matching necklace I'd made her for a birthday, the round felt coin purse with appliqued sunflowers I'd made her as a going away present just over a year ago. We're both grateful that

these few special items haven't been lost and I pack them safely away in my suitcase to keep for her until she comes home.
She gives me a pair of her shoes and a couple t-shirts (we wear
the same sizes even though she's several inches taller), keeps
a few things for herself, but most of the clothes she decides
to take downtown and share with the people she knows there,
and she uses the airbnb's washer and dryer to wash them while
James and I toss restlessly in and out of sleep in the other room.

Shyloh leaves us by the downtown public library to wait
as she takes her suitcases of freshly cleaned and folded clothes
down the block, assuring us she'll be right back. We're seated
on pretty stone benches in a small terraced courtyard, shel-
tered by a low stone wall. I peek over the wall onto the street
below, and in stark contrast to the library's tidy square is a
tightly packed row of small, tattered tents and tarps and shopping carts reaching down the entire block on both sides of the
street, people stretched out in sleeping bags or under blankets,
camped along the sidewalk, others loitering against the wall.
Strollers and carts stand precariously loaded with worldly
possessions. Some of the people are passed out or strung out,
some clearly mentally ill. There's a subtle stench of garbage,
stale liquor, urine, and cigarettes when the wind shifts toward
me. I'm immediately ashamed of my reflexive disgust at the
sight and smell, even as I'm overcome with compassion for
their situations. Many of the city's downtown homeless evi-
dently congregate here, likely for the easy access to public
bathrooms and internet and the trolley, and the city appears
exceptionally tolerant. And I realize with a jolt that this is

where Shyloh has been using the computers these past several weeks to send me messages. I struggle to imagine her on the other side of this wall, perhaps as one of those stretched out along the sidewalk, dirty and hungry, sleeping huddled under a blanket, but it's impossible for me to envision my beautiful beloved child, with all her talents and potential, as one of the seemingly forgotten people here. When she returns from distributing the clothes, I don't ask her. She'd said she wanted to protect me from the image, and I let her.

The rest of that afternoon we walk with Shyloh along the ocean, picking up shells and watching the little hermit crabs in their tidal pools. Now and then we run into people that she knows: a small group with skateboards gathered around a Hacky-Sack, music blaring from a small speaker, the smell of pot heavy in the air around them; a man ranting nonsensical verses on a street corner who stops his rant to greet her. She chats easily with him for a moment. We pass a young couple selling crafts from blankets along the boardwalk, and I can picture Shyloh there alongside them with her macrame hemp necklaces and the copper wrapped stone pendants that she loves to make. But I'm especially touched by how proudly she introduces me to all, "Hey... this is my mom!" Many of them reply with a respectful nod, and "Hey, nice to meet you," and "Oh hey, Shy talks a lot about you," and "Shy's good shit," and "You guys look alike." She is clearly adored by these new friends, and is still captivating all she meets with that contagious smile, twinkling golden green eyes, and magnetic personality. It's ironic how she is able to touch people with such absolute joy for life, when I know how broken and sad her heart is.

We stop at Tyler and Bill's the next morning to say goodbye on our way to the airport. She leaves us waiting on the sidewalk for nearly half an hour and I'm starting to get impatient and frustrated, but when she finally comes out she apologetically hands me something wrapped in a paper towel, tells me she was up all night making it for me, that she'd been waiting for the glue to dry. It's a small wooden frame; a nearly perfect sand dollar sits in the middle of the canvas, little clusters of clam and scallop shells are nestled in the corners, and she's glued a hermit crab shell to the edge, feet and eyes drawn on so it looks as though it's sneaking away. Two tiny glass vials hang from the wood border, ornately wrapped with copper wire, one filled with small chunks of mother of pearl, the other with sand. It's a cherished gift and hangs on my wall to this day. We hug with a tearful goodbye, me promising to visit again soon, she promising to write.

It has been an eye-opening visit. Holding to her promise to be honest about her drug use, Shyloh readily confessed that yes she was using but also wanted to reassure me that she was intentionally trying to limit how much. I'm not reassured and am very anxious about the choices she is making, but it helps enormously to have a clear picture in my mind of the city where she's living, to have seen and held her, to be back in regular contact with her again, and to hear her talk about coming home.

After James and I leave, Shyloh connects with Ed and

picks up her dog Rocco and over the next couple weeks she sends me pictures of the two of them, at the park snuggling in her hammock, walking along the beach, profiled against gorgeous California sunsets. It's comforting to know she has this small comrade to keep her company and I can see hints of joy and hope in her eyes.

Shyloh and Rocco, San Diego

THE ACCIDENT
– JANUARY 1, 2018

GREYHOUND BUS CRASHES IN UTAH, KILLING 13 YEAR OLD GIRL AND INJURING 11
Monday January 1, 2018

PRESS RELEASE:
I-70 Greyhound Bus Crash Update
from the DPS News, Salt Lake City, UT

On December 31, 2017 at approximately 11:00 p.m. a Greyhound bus traveling westbound from Green River went off the right shoulder of interstate 70 near mile marker 113. The bus traveled into a steep wash and came to rest approximately 200 feet off the interstate. The bus was occupied by 12 passengers and the driver. A 13-year-old female passenger was deceased on scene. The bus driver and two of the passengers were transported by air ambulance in serious condition, one to Grand Junction, Colorado and the other two to Utah Valley Medical Center in Provo. All of the other passengers except one suffered various injuries and were transported by ground ambulance to hospitals in Price and Richfield, Utah. The cause of the crash is still under investigation at this time.

Asleep on the bus seat, Shyloh is suddenly awakened with the realization she's just bounced off the bus ceiling, that the bus is falling, tumbling, crashing, then coming to a stop at the bottom of a ravine. She pushes out through the bus window and slowly picks her way up the steep slope in the dark, adrenaline and shock masking the pain and cold, finally reaching the top where the other passengers are huddled waiting for help. When help arrives, she's loaded onto the stretcher and into the helicopter.

I'm jolted awake by the ringing phone, it's 4 a.m. New Year's Day. The voice on the other end asks if I'm Andrea, if Shyloh is my daughter. Suddenly wide awake I understand that I'm speaking to someone from the emergency room in a Utah hospital, that Shyloh was on a Greyhound bus that went off the road into a ravine outside Salt Lake City. What? Wait, a bus? Utah?? My mind is frantically scrambling to make sense of what I'm hearing. The voice on the phone tells me my daughter is in stable condition but has suffered several fractured ribs, compression fractures in a couple vertebrae, a fractured shoulder blade, lung contusions, torn ligaments in her knee, a concussion. I hang up with my mind reeling and start scrambling to rearrange my work schedule and make plans to fly to Utah.

She's able to talk to me over the next couple days and I'm relieved to hear her voice, to know she'll be okay. She explains that she hitchhiked to Denver to visit Matt as a surprise, that she left Rocco with him and caught a bus back to San Diego after he told her she couldn't stay. She's clearly in shock, foggy with pain killers, and not making a lot of sense but the hospital wants to discharge her as soon as possible. I've scheduled my flight, assuming I am bringing Shyloh home with me, but without warning the nurse tells me she's been released. Shyloh calls me from a hotel in Salt Lake City the next day, tells me she was discharged with a knee brace and crutches, that Greyhound got her the room and a plane ticket back to San Diego. I plead with her to stay there and wait for me, that I'll be there tomorrow to bring her home, but she's not making sense and I'm struggling to understand what's going on, and then she's gone.

POWER OF ATTORNEY
– JANUARY 2019

Canceling my flight to Utah, I'll instead be flying to San Diego with the paperwork that will grant me power of attorney so I can manage Shyloh's personal injury case against Greyhound. I contact a recommended personal injury lawyer in Madison and explain our unique situation, that Greyhound is clearly at fault, that my daughter is currently living in California, has no address, no job, no money, no phone, compounded by her drug addictions and undiagnosed mental illness. I will need to advocate for her long distance. Miraculously, Shyloh calls during one of these meetings and, confirming that she agrees, the lawyer draws up the contract that will allow me to act on her behalf. We just need her signature.

From a borrowed phone she calls me with an address and says she'll meet me there when I get to San Diego, though it doesn't appear that she's actually staying there. She doesn't appear to be staying anywhere in particular and I speculate as to how she's managing the pain of her injuries out there on the street. My mission is to get the paperwork signed, to seek treatment for her injuries and the trauma she's endured, and to convince her to come back home with me.

When I pick her up, I'm shocked by how much weight she's lost in the month since I'd seen her last. She's twitchy and anxious, and I suspect she's "tweaking" on meth. In the past she's been careful to protect me from the worst parts of her addictions. I've not seen her like this before and it's incredibly distressing. I explain several times that I have the paperwork for her Greyhound settlement, that we need to have a notary present when she signs, and that I've found one at a FedEx nearby. She's agitated and her thinking is disorganized but she finally agrees. We get the paperwork signed and notarized. I'm relieved to have gotten this critical piece done that first day because over the next couple of days I witness Shyloh descend into a state of such erratic behavior, delusion and paranoia that we would not have been able to manage it. This is also something I'd never seen from her before and it's unclear to me how much of her behavior is due to the drugs.

I have a strong sense that the emotional trauma of the bus accident may have pushed her mind into some kind of psychotic break. Schizophrenia is the word that keeps intruding. I'm horrified and disoriented to see her like this; it appears that she's equally horrified. She makes no sense, is convinced that strangers walking down the street are listening in to our conversations through the car radio, that there are tiny secret

cameras in the trees, convinced that I know this but am playing dumb. She agrees at one point to let me take her to the
hospital, but at the intake window she refuses to give them
the necessary information, and when I explain the situation to
the nurse, I'm told that without her consent there's nothing I
or they can do.

When Shyloh passes out on my airbnb floor, I spend
hours calling hospitals and drug rehabs and hotlines. I consider calling San Diego's specialized police team, PERT
(Psychiatric Emergency Response Team), hoping they
might take her in for a seventy-two-hour hold. This is also
known as a "5150" in California, referring to the section of
their Welfare and Institutions Code that allows adults experiencing mental health crises to be detained involuntarily for
a seventy-two-hour psychiatric evaluation. They may then
receive longer term hospitalization and care, but the initial
criteria is that they must be "an immediate threat of harm
to self, harm to others, or gravely disabled." But when I do
call, the officer informs me it isn't clear that she is any of
these. It's a gamble I'm not willing to take, deciding that
unsuccessfully trying to hospitalize her by having PERT
come would likely do little more than traumatize her and
ultimately damage trust. The growing numbers of mentally
ill and addicted people living on the streets and in the parks
of San Diego have overwhelmed the few resources that have
been set up to help, and the response I get from everywhere
I call is mostly sympathetic resignation. I'm frustrated and
exhausted. A sense of helplessness is taking over.

When she wakes the next morning she seems to have calmed some and we're able to talk. She waffles on coming home with me, but finally agrees to check into Detox again and lets me call to put her name on a waitlist for inpatient rehab. We've missed this morning's check in for Detox, and because my flight home is this afternoon, Ed has agreed to let her stay with him and then take her in the next morning.

Her thinking remains a bit disorganized but she's relatively calm. We're on the curb sipping our coffees outside a nearby café waiting for Ed. As he pulls up and gets out to join us, she jumps up and takes off down the street leaving everything behind, backpack, clothes, ID, phone, and by the time I realize what's happening she's disappeared. We search and wait for hours, struggling to fathom how and why she's vanished. Eventually, though, I am forced to leave her things with Ed and, my heart heavy with worry, I head to the airport.

When I get home I spend weeks researching psychosis and schizophrenia, straining to wrap my head around what I'd just witnessed and what Shyloh was experiencing.

> *Psychosis – when the thoughts and perceptions in one's head become distorted, making it difficult to tell what is real and what is fake. People who are suffering from psychosis can hallucinate, hold onto false beliefs even when evidence disproves them, and struggle to relate to others. Someone struggling with psychosis can put themselves and others at risk because it can cause them to act erratically.*
>
> *Meth Psychosis – a psychosis that develops over*

time and is relatively common among people who struggle with meth abuse disorder, and is very similar to paranoid schizophrenia. Approximately 36.5% of methamphetamine users will develop psychosis. Hallucinations and paranoia are likely when someone is struggling with meth psychosis. Many times, one believes that the voices they hear or things they see are coming to harm them. People with meth psychosis tend to have a higher amount of paranoia. It can be difficult for a person to notice signs of psychosis in themselves because the nature of the disorder disconnects one from reality.

Drug-Induced Schizophrenia *– A recent study found that approximately 25% of people who enter a substance-induced psychosis will be diagnosed with schizophrenia. For many people who struggle with drug use, substance-induced psychosis can trigger schizophrenia. Schizophrenia normally develops in people while they are teenagers or young adults. However, it can sometimes take years to develop. Many times, schizophrenia will be in a residual stage, meaning symptoms are minor or dormant. Meth psychosis can trigger the development of active schizophrenia inside a person.*

Schizophrenia *– a chronic disorder that impacts one's brain functions. Symptoms include hallucinations, delusions, paranoia, disorganized speech, lack of movement, random hyperactivity, and a lack of motivation. If a person has a family history of psychosis or schizophrenia, they are at an even higher risk of developing the disorder if they use methamphetamines. According to the Addiction Center, nearly 50% of people with schizophrenia are dependent on either alcohol or drugs.*

ELL BEE – FEBRUARY 2018

A week later my phone buzzes at 1 a.m. I've been leaving the ringer on day and night so I won't miss her calls, but have long ago developed a reflexive dread when my phone rings, especially at night. Relief washes over me when I hear her voice on the other end and then brace myself for whatever comes next, uncertain what state of mind she'll be in or what chaos I'm about to navigate.

She tells me she'd hidden under bushes that day, off the freeway only a few blocks from where we'd been calling for her, that she'd hidden there until nightfall and then wandered until a car picked her up and she found herself in Laguna Beach, about eighty miles up the coast from San Diego. A few hours ago someone offered to let her shower and use their phone so she could call me. Her speech sounds frazzled, tired, but much more coherent than a week ago. She texts me a photo of herself, a toothy smile that doesn't quite reach her eyes, and it breaks my heart to see the pain and fragile hope and disappointment in them.

I am perpetually consumed with worry and fear for her safety. Symptoms of mania and paranoia are more and more apparent when I do hear from her, and I ruminate over whether it's the drugs or mental illness that's keeping her on the streets. I wonder if one would be easier to accept than the other; I wonder if it matters and conclude that it's likely both. I've begun to also fully recognize that this degree of addiction truly is in itself a mental illness. I simply can't wrap my head around the idea that my beautiful, talented, beloved daughter, that *anyone*, would "choose" this if they could help it.

Shyloh has found a public library in Laguna Beach and sends me an email from a new email address – *trashylitter-bugs@gmail.com* – with a pen name Ell Bee, addressed also to my folks, to her dad, and to her brother, informing us that she's decided to start a blog. Her new tags: LB, Ell Bee, Litter Bug – a play on the ladybugs she would often sign off with on holiday cards and letters when she was a child.

> **Ell Bee <trashylitterbugs@gmail.com>**
> **Feb 23, 2018, 5:54 PM**
> **SHYLOHLOVESYOUdundundunnnnnnn**
> **(drumroll) leading to semi-climactic**
> **email from SHYLOH not spam not spam**
> **spam i am yams yums sum more ... please**
>
> **************************************
> **************************************

Hey there hi there ho derr!! hehe I was trying to make it look like a junk email since this is a fresh new email of mine.

Heres the scoop on this litter bug business ... I started a blog. Mama like I told you the other day I want to be able to put your heart and everyones at rest somewhat. Seeing and knowing that I am doing something.

The challenge is now on me to actually uphold my end and stick to this. But since I like to write and need an excuse to sit still and do nothing ... this is perfect.

The blog will splain it Lucy but to sum it up, I started gathering up the trash and litter in parking lots. along sidewalks, led to alongside highways and recycling (THEY PAY YOU FOR YOUR GARBAGE HERE, California is the beesknees hehehe)

It makes me feel connected to (you guessed it) the mamabear as well as goddess Mother Earth. Even if its not appreciated or recognized it helps me feel that I have a right to be here.

I dont want to get emotional and deep but my poor little brain has reached a next level, page burner chapter that I am struggling immensely to get a hold of. I ALMOST have the usage abusage to nill but lets be honest, hard times do not a clean and easy path make. Progress tho! Spending my days focusing on trash gathering and now this bloggy thing keep my mind busy and its helping reignite the neurotransmitters that I put on ice ... literally HA

Currently I am in Laguna Beach, at the library and contemplating sticking around these parts. This weekend I am gonna take off but if things stay on the track im thinking I may just linger around this area awhile. Dana Point I want to check out, actually applied to some volunteering opportunities online. Something about Whales coming up ... im already feeling flaky as a fish fry BUT I AM DOING WHAT IVE BEEN TRYING TO DO so thats. well. that.

Please write me back and tell me tales of the land and the family and my brother bear. Does he have email? See if he would write me! and send me pointers on the blog cuz i have NO clue what I am doing. right meow its just a shell of a thing with a single post

LOVELOVELOVELOVELOVE YOU be healthy and live fully and I will see you in a few months hopefully.

Prey 4 Whirled Peas :P

Yours always, this lil ray of cali sunshyyne dreamin

Xxooxxoo

litterbugsme.wordpress.com

Though it's a little odd that picking up litter is what she's chosen to devote her time and energy to, it's not entirely out of nowhere. For several years when Shyloh and her brother were kids, I would take them up and down a two mile stretch of country road by our house each spring to collect the garbage that had accumulated there over the previous year. They each took turns driving the ATV along the shoulder, following as the other helped me fill garbage bags and load them onto the back of the four wheeler to carry home. The irony doesn't escape me here that she's now decided to clean the world, that cleaning the entire planet somehow feels less daunting than getting "clean" herself. There's also a clear manic energy apparent in her words, and from experience I begin to prepare myself for her inevitable crash within the next several weeks.

LITTERBUGSME BLOG POSTS

*A rested souls rambling
February 23, 2018 litterbugsme

The journey begins? No halo. Nor say so.
Born to breathe! Oh; struggle you mean?
YOU-ME-I'S-WE
The sun shines brighter; shadows shift
Seems lighter...BIC
But I see, I see, you me.
Satisfaction fleeting though,
      the resonance of a heart beat beaten so.
ins and outs uppers downers inside outers
Still I flick just to see the spark and flame.
undo YOUR SHAME! diffuse the blame...
re-do then games.
Or just cancel 'er if you can sir (YOU SURE?)
Surely IT was what we thought, we were.
WE. ARE.
*Today's trash...tomorrow

February 24, 2018 litterbugsme

A day in laguna beach was a true breath of fresh air. I wished a thousand times over that I had a lil fun money with all the art galleries, aromatic restaurants and wait for it; a shop devoted solely to socks! I'd like to say I overcame material greed today but had I a dollar to spare, a pair of knee highs might have gone on layaway. HEHE

As always I'm a hungry caterpillar, emotions rolled over me in fuchsia tidal waves. Why pink? No rhyme just the feeling. At days end the last wink of the day recalls memories of life love and family. To yours, count the good vibes sent; to mine the same plus all my love sprinkled with a hint of pizazz (mainly cuz I'm thinking of my mama and her hubby making home cooked thin crust pizza) NOMNOM-NOM *LOVE YOU MAMABEAR*

Smooches, night all!

February 24, 2018 litterbugsme

Pizza on my mind, extra. Cheesy. Not so saucy.
  Ode to the crust! Thick or thin no matter, either
  or impress upon me.
Or upon my stomach rather. The guts. The Core.
(Heres the split)
  Right? To the core of the earth, it's LIVE the
  heat, firey light
Eyes burn, sore 'for the sight.
Crust of our Mother Earth is heavy... Gravity.
Downtrodden our people ARE. Confused? Bye
and by the depravity...
The depraved should pay, but who?!
That's no easy call;
Line up on the wall, wake up, wake 'em all.
By the toll of a bell far off, distant.
Reminiscent.
Let us de-pave in stead, prey for better, tomorrow.
Flower children and that whole raquet.
Hands in hand- ahh, peace...
Peace pipe? Pack it!
Now we REALLY need that 'za.
When this dream ends I'll bake one for yah.

CAGED – MARCH 2018

I receive a call from Las Colinas Women's Detention Center informing me Shyloh has been arrested for felony auto theft, and that she's in jail awaiting arraignment. I feel like I have chronic emotional whiplash. She asked that they call to let me know she's okay but won't be able to call me herself until after she's been arraigned, which has been delayed for a week due to her mental state. She's refusing to get on the bus that will take her to the courthouse, and they're holding her in the jail's medical ward. I'm told she's been crying inconsolably since she got there.

This crime is so out of character. She's arraigned and released until her court date on her own recognizance. When she does finally call she tells me she'd seen the keys lying on the counter in a laundromat, found the car and hopped in, that she'd been so very tired, tired of walking, tired of being cold and hungry, that it was merely a welcomed opportunity. I believe her, I know there was no true criminal intent, but I can only think this is a blessing in disguise: forced detox, intervention, relatively safe, fed. But still, it breaks my heart.

I'm so sad. All the time, just sad, and nothing I can do but keep moving forward, do the next thing and finally the day is over, repeat.

Once she's been sentenced, I'll be able to settle into whatever the next phase is, hoping she gets enough time in jail to get detoxed and clean, to get psychiatric help. And I'm hoping for at least a year plus mandatory rehab and counseling, hoping she'll at least receive professional grief and trauma support. I am preparing to visit once we know her long term situation, and already looking into flights and rooms.

She picks back up with her blog postings, signing off regularly now with variations of her new tag, eLBe or LB, short for LitterBug:

LitterBugsMe Blog Posts

*Picking up trash in dresses
March 9, 2018 litterbugsme
WOAH! What a journey I have been on, my litter buggyness led me down a dark path for a brief moment in time. Looking for a break and I caught arrest! I am no angel, just a gypsy seeking change, sometimes you get a wooden nickel though and well I found myself under lock and key for a few days.
I have not given up my desire to keep striving towards a cleaner tomorrow, starting today;

each day. It will take me another deep breath or two (or three) to regain momentum on my path to cleanliness but fear not readers, litter still bugs me.

~eLBe

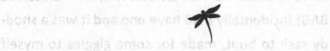

Jail gave me a little of my gumption back, no time to lose succombing to the will of those who do not have my best interest in mind. No more fretting over rejection (ok a little fretting) and wrapping self inside self. FLY BE FREE LITTER BUG just pick up when youre done

I love you. Yes, you. This moment this miracle thank the Goddess for her blessings, I feel the heat of her beat in my chest.

RESPECT YOUR MOTHER.

-eLBe outttt

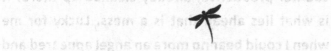

March 11, 2018 litterbugsme

*As close to the border of Mexico as you can get without a rifle in your face. That is where my morning began. Awkward sleeping situations led me to my fail safe; when in doubt walk that shit OUT!

And a littering I shall go

It was 4am when I started mustering the sense of direction for my day. Snacks in my pack? CHECK Head on straight? ... at least on shoulders? CHECK Supplies necessary for highway clean up? ... HOW HARD TO REMEMBER A DAMN GARBAGE BAG! Incidentally I did have one and it was a shoddy sack to boot, made for some giggles to myself throughout the day indeed and Mother Earth was in support for my actions as every time I would come to the end of the sack stuffing abilities another bag would appear under a rock or hooked to a tree branch. I will never fully understand how the worlds majesty can be so simplex but let it never be said I don't appreciate the magick.

I didnt realize but I walked Hwy 94 for nearly 9hrs. In the rain, midday but once you go so far it only makes sense to continue in a forward motion. Turning around would have been counter productive; already cleaned up there! it is what lies ahead that is a mess. Lucky for me when I could bear no more an angel appeared and whisked me to my start point in their beefy pickup. Much appreciated, thank you JA   your good deeds are reciprocated with good vibes. xxo

To the would be litter bug:

MAKE SURE TO STRETCH

AND DRINK WATER!

Two most essential bits of wisdom appli-

cable to all things Life but especially for manual labor. I am a solo garbage harvester so I lug the trash bag on my own, hit both sides of the street, manage my own breaks and snacks etc. If only I could get paid to do this!!

It is hard not to panic reading this account and imagining everything else that's happened to her that she hasn't shared. But I'm grateful at least that she's survived to relate this particular adventure. And as always, having a picture in my mind – no matter how distressing – helps to ease the not knowing.

I smile ruefully at the little private jokes that I know she is sending straight to me. In my competitive boxing days, I'd become a strong proponent of staying hydrated, and because I was constantly working out and sweating I would often drink a gallon or more of water daily. Whenever Shyloh or Zeke would come to me with some minor physical complaint, I would remind them to stretch and drink plenty of water. It soon became a running joke that whenever there was ANYTHING wrong, the solution was "don't forget to stretch and drink water!"

*Inspired aspiring entrepreneur etc…
March 15, 2018 litterbugsme
Social anxieties are still upending at times

but time is proving that sticking to what I know works and focusing on true positivity is building self confidence, endurance and relationships with community members throughout the San Diego area.

When the litter bug came to me as a coping mechanism to tolerate the emotional pain that tends to shroud me in solitude it was something to concentrate on when I feel unsafe in any way. The whole idle hands thing ya know? Now I find myself stressing out when I DON'T pick up litter as I pass it! Ha not all bad I suppose plus its perfect for my ODD perspectives as I am inadvertently utilizing reverse psychology on myself.

At any rate. Life is live and constantly springing tests and lessons and worst of all directions (I will never learn to walk the walk but I sure can walk. period.

Words of WIZEDUMB to fellow litter bugs:

Remember your physical health, I am a hypocrite, always overdue it and end up with swollen knees and a sore...everything BUT knowing the appropriate warm ups cool downs and maintenance throughout every day is essential to physical comfort.

Snacks. Snacks. Snacks...wash your hands first though.

To my family, always sending you love missing you thinking and fretting and dreaming. You know me mostest and all my good deeds stem from the home base so MWAH...Im gonna keep the blame for the fuckery on myself just cuz I am a glutton for punishment hehe

Pledging loyalty to Mother Earth and devoting what I can of myself to treating her the way she deserves; YOU GET WHAT YOU PUT INTO THE WORLD, ideally.

-eLBe

*crackin' Whys...persona update
March 16, 2018 litterbugsme
WHY DO I LBM?
-eco-friendly movement
-LITTER ACTUALLY DOES BUG ME
-necessity to cope with panic attacks and restructuring coping mechanisms
I AM
-a compass that doesn't point north, lost and wandering, seeking only the next step and to tread on my sole alone.
-I DO need help but am not helpless
-small goal; big aspirations **lipstick on the mirror. keep it simple stooped**MWAH
-motivated to regain stability, forces of MY nature ride against the grain
-shaping THIS i seek UNITY

SENTENCED – MARCH-NOV 2018

I'm thankful that I can check in on her daily through her blog posts, these glimpses into her thoughts and wanderings. And then she does it again, "borrows" a car without the owner's permission, and is arrested for a second felony auto theft. This time they don't let her out.

She's sentenced to sixteen months but will only serve nine. She requests no early release, confides in fact that she doesn't want to ever leave. But because she's declined early release, there will be no mandatory rehab or counseling attached. She says she doesn't trust herself to follow through with any release requirements, that she wants to be free and clear once her time is done. I understand but don't agree; it's disappointing that we won't be able to take better advantage of the situation to get as much help as possible, for as long as possible.

Shyloh and I write to each other almost daily and send the accumulated letters in thick envelopes at the end of each week.

I schedule weekly phone calls, and once I figure out how to do video visits we eagerly log on once a week to giggle and beam at each other. As strange as it may seem, these months are the most content either of us has been for a long time, both of us relishing the relative security jail is offering her.

Supporting an incarcerated loved one can get expensive, and I'm constantly loading money onto her commissary and phone accounts. But I just can't resist when she calls and pleads from time to time for something special.

"The granola package, please??? And maybe the one that has the chocolate too? Numnumnum!" When I occasionally balk, she reminds me we're "borrowing" from her eventual settlement with Greyhound, which is slowly being negotiated. I'm told it could be another year before they settle.

It's prison-time:o'clock somewhere.
Sketched by LB (Shyloh)

(poem Shyloh wrote and sent from jail)

<u>One Crazy Life</u>
No matter what we're dealt, just play the game
It's not about winning- hashtags for fame?
That's fucking lame!
Anyways...
This is it- Breathe- it is this
Painfully simplex yet complex to the max
I'll take the max. No paper. No parole
Show your hand, let em see the dice roll
Dueces! No- aces high, reach for the sky
Roll with the punches. Fuck takebacks or relapse
Live Love Laugh 'til your lungs collapse
This one crazy life is all we're given
If all bets were off, all sins forgiven
Tell me, now how you feel about livin'? - LB

I fly out to visit for her birthday, which is also Mother's Day weekend. The jail's waiting room is filling up with expectant family members, some with small children fidgeting restlessly to see mothers or siblings. Others, like me, are mothers here to see daughters. Many of the women locked up with Shyloh are here for petty drug crimes; many are addicts and/or mentally ill.

She's put on some weight now that she's eating regularly, and the antipsychotics and mood stabilizers she's on may also be contributing. She looks and sounds good, though, and she excitedly tells me about her plans to come home after her release, to finish college, to start over again. She tells me she's been journaling daily and mentions she's considering writing a book about her experiences and asks if I would help her. She's always had a way with words and is so creative, and I encourage all of it. Smiling, she tells me she's made me something for my birthday/mother's day, and hands me a tiny booklet made from scraps of paper, bound with thread. She's carefully composed small sketches in the corner of each page so that the drawings come to life as I let the pages flip quickly through my fingers. My eyes well up as I watch a tiny seed become a seedling, then grow tall. As a purple bloom emerges, a ladybug crawls up the flower's stalk and a butterfly flies in from the edge of the page to hover while "Happy Birthday" scrolls along the top. Each small page depicts so much care and love. Obviously, the circumstances could be better, but I am so relieved to have my daughter back that I hardly mind the armed guards that interrupt our goodbye hug.

(poem Shyloh wrote and sent from jail)

Choices

Standing – a crossroads
Make like a tree and leave?
Bat outta hell
Racing- no reprieve
Talking- thoughts, it's all in your head
Only YOU know what is said
Stuck- feet are lead
Not all of us get to walk both ways
Split- thru the multiverse
One runs. One stays.
Choices, choices
Listen- to the voices
Choose- you know what's true

Sketched by LB (Shyloh)

ON THE FENCE

Shyloh is doing writing exercises from one of the work-books I'd given her, *The Wisdom to Know the Difference* by Wilson and DuFrene, and sends me her work in a large ma-nila envelope, written in pencil on lined, yellow paper.

In one exercise she's asked to write about two memories she will never forget:

Unforgettable moments- My mom has always be-lieved that each moment we truly experience becomes a part of us. I tend to agree with her on most things, this is no exception. Every single little detail leading up to right now, even as I move this pencil across this paper, is equally precious. It has to be or I could never love myself as I do today. Compassion towards who I am (to the core) has been my life's struggle. I can look back across my life's timeline and highlight key events, sure, but depending on my mood that day, or what purpose the exercise serves-flagged moments could change continuously. Many things I've tried (and failed) to forget. The darkest corners of my psych are riddled with ugly memories where I play victim and villain alike. Unforgettable? Damn skippy. Worthy of mention? Not hardly. There are a lot of great experiences too tho. My life has been one epic adventure to say the least! I'll always remember how it felt to leap from a perfectly good airplane. It is a moment frozen in time for sure, celebrating sobriety, loving life, my parents still together... as I write about this a flood of emotions is overcoming me. A reel of similarly exceptional moments spent both with my family and without. Waves of sorrow and guilt- damn near nauseous from it all. This, coupled with passionate love for my mom and my dad, who truly love me and want what is best for me; I can't pick just a couple events cuz in 30 yrs I've appreciated and been blessed with, well, 30 yrs of LIFE! Even in the throws of addiction I would pause and marvel at the absolute beauty of a sunrise, or a meteor shower amidst the northern lights, seen from my tent in MN backcountry. I saw a point from a hillside that showed the curvature of the Earth. The world laid out below me, stretching endlessly. Then 10 miles later my backpacking days were over as I blew out my knee. So to me? Every memory, all the combined seconds of my existence are each drops of water into an everflowing river. One droplet may seem meaningless, or it may be the one to erode away a bit of stone at the river bottom. I value all of it, the good and bad, the past and future.

Another exercise asks her to notice places in her life where she has been absent or less present. She has chosen Education & Learning:

These recent months have been the only time in a long while I've felt passionate, focused, undeterred from expanding my mind with no objective other than simply to do so. School always came easy to me but even before the drugs took priority I'd always craved "streetwise", I wanted to LEARN all the "bad girl" shit, and wanted to prove I could have both my education and a dark past, that I could be a functioning addict. If I imagine an actual fence line between two pastures, in order to maintain the land on either side I have to pick one and venture in. I feel like I've been squatting on the fence most of my life, afraid to pick a side, unwilling to recognize that I could circle back when I was ready. These past years I finally jumped into the mud and tramped right into the thick. The pasture I'd chosen was overgrown and dangerous AF! I just barely made it back to the fence, damn near killed myself exploring THAT side. The grass was way greener in some spots, but there were some really barren patches too. I'm glad to have gone there and to have learned it first hand. I've craved that understanding for so long. I'm not sated yet but I'm back on the fence, gazing out across the yet to be seen wonders of the other side. I feel so thirsty and the well of deep understanding and fucking serenity is just down from where I now rest, not even out in the middle, I CAN SEE IT FROM HERE! I'm loving this analogy and the little sketch I did, and the ease at which I'm processing this shit is proof to myself of how far I've come. I can always change course, but I can't REALLY learn anything if I don't get off the fence.

As her release date looms, she wonders if she should wean off her medications while she's in jail, to see if she's able to do without them. Her reasoning: what if she can't manage her prescription once she's out, can't find someone to write it, to fill it, to pay for it? I wonder too if she feels the medications have deadened her spark, will dull the wits she knows she'll need once on the "outs." She's confident though that she no longer needs the medications, and though I'm strongly opposed to the idea, I agree that if she's going to do it, it makes sense that she do it while monitored in a protected environment. But I'm not able to speak to her therapist because of privacy laws, so I have no way of knowing if they are aware of her plans or if she's stopped taking the meds on her own. It's not long before I notice a manic quality to her voice. She misses several of our scheduled video visits because she's been put on lockdown for disruptive behavior. The handwriting in her letters is almost illegible at times, the messages bounce more and more towards erratic and nonsensical, and she has begun drawing conclusions between concepts that have no connections. I'm trying hard not to worry; she'll be home soon and we can manage whatever needs managing then.

(poem Shyloh wrote and sent from jail)

Breathe
There$ a ringing in my ear$
my viion going red
Focu$ing on my breathing
$o I don't rip off your head
Muscle$ tight
Fight or flight
Ain't no happy ever after
Pick and choo$e
To win or lo$e
My life'$ a natural di$a$ter
Inhale.
Exhale.
Mindful repetition
I keep tryin'- $o I don't fail
$lowly, clearing my vi$ion - LB

Done - Easily - Undone
Sketched by LB (Shyloh)

RELEASE – NOVEMBER 11, 2018

Initially we plan to meet as she walks out the prison doors, both of us imagining the moment as from a movie scene, and then we'll fly back home together where family and close friends can help her get back on her feet. She discusses with me her plans of finishing her degree and taking writing classes with the hopes of one day writing a book about her struggles. I make arrangements to get her into grief and trauma counseling, decorate our guest room for her and equip it with a writing desk, notebooks and sketch pads, pens and colored pencils. But as the reality of her impending freedom looms, her courage starts to waver. She argues with me during her final weeks of confinement that she needs to "say goodbye to Cali" before heading back to "Sconnie," her nickname for Wisconsin.

"Just for a week or so," she assures me. She'll stay with Ed until just after Thanksgiving and then be home for Christmas. My heart sinks even as I hold onto fragile hope that it will all pan out. It doesn't. Her sobriety lasts less than forty-eight hours and she's again on the roller coaster of diluting the shame of her addiction with more drugs.

She has a phone but no phone service, so she messages friends and family through Facebook Messenger when she's able to find wifi. She starts right back into her blog posting as LB, no mention of prison, as though the past nine months had only been a hiccup.

I am grateful to be able to maintain a connection to her days through her blog posts and am often able to get a read on her mental state. Her behavior and writing are increasingly manic, but again it isn't clear whether it's directly drug induced or something more organic or, and most probably, a combination of the two.

More LitterBugsMe blog posts.

*SIMPLE SHIT MY FRIENDS.
Respect your mother.
November 17, 2018 litterbugsme

Litter is an issue, and not just cuz I'm complaining about it, who else loves our earth Mother? I'm going to start by encouraging everyone to just (please for the literal preservation of our world) just. dispose. accordingly.

To the lady on the street next to me yesterday: don't leave your hipster Chobani yogurt container in a bush along the sidewalk like it's !want as a gift. Are you serious? THERE WAS A TRASH CAN

AT THE CORNER UP THE HILL. Even if there was no can, your backpack was not so nice it couldn't risk a rogue drop of yogurt from your snack cup. How can you think yourself to be so, SO [I CAN'T FIND THE WORDS] SO ENTITLED [yes, that checks out] that you can't possibly manage an empty container; even though you just ate the damn thing while walking your bike.…

Hey don't trip tho! I scooped it up behind you and tossed it out proper. and it was a good deed on MY day; Lord knows I need the bonus points to keep the balance.

Back to Ranting

Trash is absolutely everywhere! The neighborhood demographic is easy to see based solely on the litter laying around. some of that I'm sure has to do with paying people to clean the streets of the high-speed communities and those home owners and spending a lot to live as they do so they are doubtful to dump their freshly used condom at the end of the driveway. (EWW) Head to the more highly populated regions and you'll find what you've been missing. Yeah, I'm talking about all that rotting festering junk piled into alleys and choking out those pathetic office gardens.

> **Quick sidenote: I once spent 5hrs cleaning around two dumpsters behind an Office Max in downtown San Diego and the thanks I got was to find my backpack to be stolen and I ripped my shoe beyond repair…BUT OHHMYGAWD IT WAS SO SATISFYING TO SEE A JOB WELL DONE. there was human feces, and syringes and broken glass, expired food… But to know I could be preventing a grave mishap and providing a clean slate for the surrounding area was rad and I'd do it again in a heartbeat.**

There is such absurdity to what she's described here, and I recoil at these shared details, yearning to picture her walking along roadsides with her plastic bags instead, picking up old food containers, wrappers, bottles and newspapers. I wonder at her efforts to "clean" this disgusting example of human filth. If this alley scene, which few will ever witness, has become her norm.

The frenzied blog posts continue.

> ***Yes, I talk about garbage, alot, hence the blog…are you actually confused?***
> **November 17, 2018 litterbugsme**
> Litter bugs me is my little dream and it's already in reality because I have wandered along city streets, backcountry roads and freeways collecting as much non-biodegradable materials as I can tote along with me. So far I am an army of one; except

this one night a guy named Jared offered me some pizza and followed me for a few hours...if he hadn't been handsome and age appropriate it may have been really creepy.

Back on track tho I work alone and I'm perfectly fine to do so. I encourage any enthusiasts to please grab a bag and gloves and gather up the cigarette butts or old lotto tickets. Giving ANY measurement of time provides immediate relief to our environment and will cause warm fuzzies inside of you (to clarify, warm fuzzies is not some trash borne contagion. IT'S THEM LOVING GOOD VIBES). I'm at times where I had nothing but a dingy pack on my shoulder, no money to spare, I would go to establishments that would have the material I require to do this self-appointed job. Gloves and trash bags and in a perfect world? Hand sanitizer...

ohhmygawd it's a pretty disgusting process despite the feel goods and activism, there is a part of me that is totally grossed out that I do this, REGULARLY. and I share the whole ordeal on social media (gasp). But I then think, to that snobby piece of my brain, that it'll be way embarrassing if the fucking earth explodes or shrivels up and we all waste away in miserable, varying stages of decay and then ALL OF A SUDDEN we are the litter, just looking gross and unwanted, used up and of no value. Ouch, kinda harsh...sorry NOT SORRY. Do your part man...

**well, I'll do mine ... Making change without breaking
the river in your pocket. Every day throw something
away.**

She calls briefly from Ed's on Thanksgiving, having
stopped by to shower and eat. Ed had bought her plane ticket back to Wisconsin; her flight is in two days. She chirps
cheerily, "Happy Turkey Day! Don't worry, I'll see you soon,
Mama Bear!" But the day of her flight comes and goes and
I wonder about the bottomlessness of certain things and how
my heart can continue to sink. She shows up to Ed's the following day and calls me, sobbing, apologizing over and over
that she'd lost track of the days and I can hear a part of her
starting to let go – the part of her that wants desperately to
please, the part that's so very tired of trying to live up to expectations and potentials, of feeling like a disappointment to
those she loves.

I believe there are pearls of truth to the things she tells
me, that she means what she says when she says it, and I hold
tightly to this, but it's so hard to know what to truly believe,
how to keep holding on to a relationship so entwined with
the selfishness of addiction. I recognize that I could put up a
self-protective wall and shut her and all her chaos out completely as so many people do with their addicted and mentally
ill loved ones. But then I would lose her altogether, and I'm
not willing to do this. I struggle with this dichotomy daily.
Is it worth holding on at all costs when sometimes I'm not

even sure who it is I'm talking to? When she reaches out to me, high and/or manic and consumed with her conspiracies or grand plans, I'm often at a loss for how to respond. I strain for glimpses of the daughter I love so dearly. I get angry and frustrated, and then I regret having missed another opportunity to gain understanding. I keep asking her to agree to get help, pleading with her that it doesn't have to be like this, that I love her, that so many people love her, that I miss the Shyloh that I knew, that I don't know how to talk to her when she's like this.

"What if I'm always going to be like this, Mama?" she sobs. "What if this is me? Will you just stop talking to me?" and another piece of my heart breaks away. Of course I will continue to hold on. It's all so complicated, but I know without a doubt that, somehow, I will figure out how to navigate this.

I've sustained several injuries lately that are keeping me from my regular trail runs, my main outlet for stress, and I notice as a result I've been drinking more than usual; an occasional glass of wine after dinner has become two every night. I desperately need a way to shut my mind off. I've been leaving my phone on at night in case she calls, and I haven't been sleeping. My heart leaps out of my chest every time it rings.

Shyloh resumes her blog.

*A promising start to the years end
December 4, 2018 litterbugsme
Reactions from people in passing has been
positive and for a fledgling movement these interac-

tions really do a lot to keep motivated. From an outsider perspective I imagine the image might be odd– me with a backpack strapped on tight, nitrile gloves, trash bag in hand. Keeping a cheery disposition is going to go far in all of this, and the struggle gets real but practice makes perfect practices right? Haha

On a personal note? The very scatterbrained beginnings of this blog and overall mission have finally begun to take shape and while I have much growth as an entrepreneur to expect I actually have a passion. This is my sidebar goal as Litter Bug, to create sustainable satisfaction as a member of this world. Some of the bigger hurdles to get by now:

-buy the domain name
-draft donation request letter
-expand demographic

CRAZY PEOPLE – JANUARY 2019

There's been no activity on her blog page for weeks, and she is no longer replying to Facebook messages. And because nobody knows where she is or how to get in touch with her, there's nothing to do but wait and hope she calls.

Another month goes by when the San Diego police call to inform me she's been picked up on a 5150. The officer tells me neighborhood residents had been calling in complaining Shyloh was knocking on their doors asking for water and acting "crazy." She was taken to Bayview Behavioral Health Hospital and she'd asked the police to let me know. I'm guessing she's had a psychotic break, either organic or meth induced, and I'm told by the hospital that she is heavily medicated and relatively stable. I want to go immediately, but know I should wait. She won't be able to talk to me for a while anyway with all those meds in her system. It's nearly two weeks before she's finally able to call me herself.

She tells me she doesn't like how the meds make her feel and that she has gained fifteen pounds already. I think to myself she could use the weight; she had gotten so painfully thin.

At 5'8" she's easily a healthy, fit 140 pounds, but was about 115 pounds when police picked her up. She also complains that she's surrounded by "all these crazy people."

But it's so good to talk to her, to have her sound more like my Shyloh, to have logical threads return to our conversations.

She agrees to sign a release of information so the doctors can share information with me, and I'm told she's been given a tentative diagnosis of *bipolar-type schizoaffective disorder.* This disorder presents as a combination of symptoms of schizophrenia and bipolar mood disorder, including delusions, hallucinations, depressed episodes and manic periods of high energy, and cycles of severe symptoms that are often followed by periods of improvement. This description seems to fit. She tells me she's finally ready to come home and I make arrangements to fly out and get her as soon as the doctors determine she's ready to leave. Then without any warning from the hospital staff, I'm told she's no longer there. The doctor informs me that she stopped taking her medication several days ago, and has checked herself out.

I've been told over and over by the police that it's not illegal to be homeless, to be mentally ill, and ironically, though drug use is illegal, it's not illegal to be an addict. Unless she's an "immediate danger to herself or others," they can't forcefully detain her beyond the initial seventy-two-hour hold if she chooses not to be there. They can't force her to take the medications; she's an adult after all.

I try to argue, "... but OF COURSE she's a danger to herself!" These drugs she can't help shooting into her veins are a kind of protracted suicide. And her mental illness prevents her from seeking help even when she's trying valiantly to dry out. It's an infuriating circular argument. How can a person who, because they're mentally ill and don't believe they need help, choose to get help?

And so, she's gone again.

I throw myself into boxing. Several years ago a good friend helped me start a nonprofit to provide financial support for the amateur boxing program I now run. The money raised helps to fund travel and lodging for my boxers and myself for national tournaments, as well as providing gym memberships and boxing gear for kids who can't afford them. I call them "kids," but most of them are technically adults, roughly the same age as my own children. I find a comforting irony in this detail. This year our nonprofit has assumed the responsibility of hosting an annual state tournament and will be taking our state's champions to compete nationally as a team. It's nearly overwhelming trying to focus on keeping all the plates spinning to pull it off, but I do. In fact, I suspect it's the all-consuming nature of the tasks that keep me moving forward each day. I've been practicing this moving forward through chaos for years after all.

My birthday comes and goes, then Mother's Day, then Shyloh's birthday, occasions that have always held a special place for both Shyloh and myself and have previously never gone unobserved by either of us. I can't help but imagine the worst. I file another missing person report with San Diego police and California Missing Persons.

I am embroidering on one of Shyloh's old hoodies that she'd left when she first went to San Diego. I chose to decorate it with the sunflowers that have always reminded me of her, and the words of a mantra I've recently taken up, "May you be happy; may you be at ease; may you be safe; may you be free from suffering." I use the time I work on it to cry, to think about her, to miss her, to send these words to her through space. And then I put it away; I put my thoughts of her and my heartache away so I can function in my world for the rest of the day. Holding onto the belief that I'll see her again, I decide to give it to her when it's finished.

One morning in June, I wake to a notification on my phone. It's a Facebook message from a name I don't recognize but something prods me to check it anyway. This stranger named Miguel says he knows Shyloh, he'd seen her picture on a Facebook post by California Missing Persons listing my name and contact info. He and a couple other people have been looking out for her since she moved into their area several weeks ago, checking in on her every few days. He tells me he is homeless too, and that he also has a daughter, and I'm touched to hear how this community seems to care for its own. He says Shyloh has the most beautiful eyes he's ever seen and I agree, she does, golden hazel like a lioness's. Most everyone that meets Shyloh for the first time will comment on her eyes.

He sends me the spot on Google Maps – Spring Valley, California, just outside San Diego. "It's down the block from the 7-11. There's a wall along the sidewalk. About halfway down the block the wall ends and there's some bushes, and she stays in there." He tells me she seems very sad, and that she would be so angry at him if she knew he'd told anyone where she was, that she gets in "these moods," and so he doesn't let her know that he's told her mom where she is. But I'm thankful he at least has access to a phone, and I contact him nearly every day to make sure she's still there, that she's okay.

This news fills me with renewed hope and energy. I pull up the spot on my computer and go to satellite view, then street view. I move the computer mouse down the block, along the wall. Tears of release flow as I find the end of the wall and see the bushes, part of me imagining I'll see her there. I don't, of course, but now I have a place to direct my thoughts. I book my flight and will those two weeks to speed by faster, afraid of what can happen to plans and fragile hopes when left too long. Several times a day I pull up that street view on my computer and imagine her there.

FORT UNICORN – JULY 2019

Spring Valley, California

When I get off the plane at San Diego International, I drive straight to her. I memorized the route from Google Maps. I park my rental car at the 7-11 and start moving down the block, along the wall as it had been described to me, for the first time and yet so familiar. Time slows down. The smells and sounds imprint on my mind, yet I barely remember the walk itself. And then I'm at the end of the wall and there are the bushes I'd seen from my computer screen. It feels unreal seeing them in front of me and knowing I'm about to move beyond them. I see a narrow footpath leading into the brush. She doesn't know I've come to find her.

As I move up the path I call her name, first tentatively then louder, and suddenly I hear "Mama???" and see her astonished face coming up the path towards me.

We hold each other and cry and laugh. I can't believe I have her in my arms. She too is overwhelmed, and it takes us both a while to settle into the reality of it as she shows me around her camp.

She's named her space Fort Unicorn, and she, the Duchess of Knothing.

Shyloh and her mom

Our first day together is incredibly intense, wonderful, and emotionally exhausting. We go for a walk, and laugh and giggle and marvel at the amazing flora of southern California, at the flowers and trees here that seem to have come out of a Dr. Seuss book. Shyloh tells me Dr. Seuss lived in San Diego and we agree these plants must have influenced his imaginative illustrations. She'd gotten a tattoo on her calf several years ago of a Truffula tree from *The Lorax*, one of our favorite Seuss books when she was a kid, and also tattooed a quote from the story: "Unless someone like you cares a whole awful lot, Nothing is going to get better. It's not." I wonder which heartbreak led her to have this inked into her skin. I think of asking but the moment passes.

I give her the embroidered hoodie with the sunflowers and mantra, describing how I worked on it during those months when I didn't know where she was, how I would hold her in my mind while I worked, sending my love through space from my heart to hers. She tells me how she would send me messages through space too and we vow to pay attention to those moments in the future when you suddenly feel the other's love, convinced we must be connected by some cosmic thread. She shares with me some of her writings, poems and sketches and asks me to hold onto them for her so she doesn't lose them, and I stow these small windows into her heart and mind protectively away in my small backpack.

But as the stress and excitement of the day begin to wear on both of us, her mental state starts to degrade. She's arguing with voices only she hears and is barely talking directly to me anymore. She doesn't believe that I don't hear them too. I don't know how to respond to this. It's strange and scary and I feel disoriented. She's also convinced that cameras are hidden in the trees around the camp, in the surrounding neighborhood, that "they're" watching us. After several hours of her paranoid ramblings she announces that she needs a break, she's got a busy schedule, she hadn't known I was coming, do I expect her to suddenly drop everything?

I want to respect her space. I tell her I love her, that I'm staying nearby, and will be back in the morning.

"I love you too, Mama." We hold each other in a long, teary hug, then say goodnight. I'm exhausted and secretly relieved to escape for a while.

I drive to Walmart to buy her a phone and set it up for her. Then I drive to a nearby nature reserve with running trails. I go for a hard run and am finally hit fully by the emotions of the day.

Over the next week I'm with her in the mornings and afternoons. I ask her about her days and nights, and she tells me about her evening routine of dumpster diving to collect cans and look for food, of the interesting things she finds. It is amazing actually what people throw away. The money from recycling cans she uses to buy bottled water, an occasional morning coffee, cigarettes, a can of beer or wine, laundry. The guy who works at the 7-11 likes her and saves her all the leftover doughnuts from the day before instead of throwing them out. And there's a couple other people, Miguel for one, who stay in the area and come through to check on her now and then, bringing her food and sometimes cigarettes or a little cash from selling stuff that she finds. I suspect they bring her drugs too.

She's newly obsessed with drawing elaborate ambigrams, words that are drawn to look the same when flipped or reversed, and has sketches of them everywhere. Her most recent one is of her brother's name, Zeke. And there are also variations of her new graffiti tag AsF, short for *As Fuck*, and its morphed version ACE. I notice she's now signing most of her poems and artwork with ACE instead of LB, or Shyloh.

She's been collecting electrical cords and stripping the insulation for the silver and copper wire; with it she wraps shells and stones to make pendants. She tells me she's even sold a few. They are pretty, some are excellent, though I can see her overactive mind in the over-elaborate wrappings of others. She's always been imaginative and I'm not surprised at these creations, but I can't help imagining all she could be doing with her talent and creativity if only… I hate this line of thinking though.

Mostly we sit in her camp and try to communicate, and I try to hold on to my own sanity. I help pull the insulating plastic off the cords.

At first she's reluctant to accept the phone. But when I do step away to give us both a break, we text and call each other, and I can tell she loves having me close even as she struggles when we're together. I love being able to make contact with her easily with the phone after so many months without knowing where or how she was. And though it's heartbreaking, I'm so grateful to be near when she calls me in the night seeking comfort.

We are sitting quietly together on the worn loveseat, watching the ants filing purposefully towards the tarp entangled cooler, and witnessing the snails climb inexplicably up the trees into the hot sun where they're slowly roasted to death. I comment on the Hello Kitty headband she's wearing, the Hello Kitty fingerless gloves, the cracked Hello Kitty coffee cup placed at one of her small "shrines," never having known her to be a fan of anything Hello Kitty. She proceeds to tell me a story, one of the only stories she's shared with me about the bus accident.

Asleep on the bus seat, she describes how she's suddenly awakened with that feeling of falling. Impossibly she realizes she's just bounced off the bus ceiling, that they really are falling, tumbling, crashing, the bus finally coming to a stop at the bottom of the ravine, the lifeless body of the thirteen year old girl who'd been in the seat across the aisle lying crumpled across her own. She tells me how she pushes out from under the girl and crawls out the bus window and makes her way up the side of the ravine in the dark, adrenaline and shock masking the pain and cold. Finally reaching the top, she realizes she's gone up the wrong side of the ravine and slowly struggles her way back down towards the bus. Now she's freezing. At the bus again, she crawls in through the window looking for something to protect against the cold. Finding nothing else, she takes the jacket from the dead girl's body. Back out through the window, she fights her way up the other side of the ravine toward the road where the other passengers are huddled waiting for help. As she's loaded onto the stretcher and into the helicopter, she vaguely recalls feeling a lump against her side. Later, in the hospital, when her clothes are returned to her, she discovers the girl's Hello Kitty doll in the jacket's pocket.

She tells me she can't stop thinking about the girl, has nightmares about her, consumed with guilt for taking the jacket, for surviving.

I'm convinced that this horrific experience has contributed to her altered mental state and am newly committed to finding a way to convince her to accept help in processing this grief and trauma. If only she would come home with me. I wonder what options there are right now, here, for getting help for Shyloh, if she would accept help if I could find any.

I'm struggling to find something I can do that's helpful. I mention several times that I can help her with the laundry she keeps mentioning and fretting about. Or maybe it's me that's fretting. I've got the rental car after all, and I want to save her the struggle of hauling the laundry up the block. And so that afternoon I sit with her as she goes through one of the huge piles of clothes at the edge of her camp. I try to be patient and only observe, but it's obvious these clothes are not hers, that some have been there for a very long time, many of them are in rotting tatters, and most of them won't even fit her. My mind keeps trying to wrap itself around what she is doing and why, but she gets agitated when I ask. Eventually we have a new pile of relatively salvageable clothes, and we bag them into several garbage bags. I decide not to ask anymore; I'll help get them to the laundromat.

My visit's coming to an end. I've been here just over a week and will be leaving in two days. I doubt she'll be coming home with me. I'm anxious that time is running out to get anything meaningful done for her while I'm here. I've been visiting and calling hospitals, homeless outreach, addiction rehabs and mental health clinics, desperately trying to find help. Since her stay in Bayview, I've been laboriously researching schizophrenia and other psychotic disorders and learned that extreme emotional and physical trauma can push a mind already heritably predisposed over the edge, and so I try to explain to everyone I call about the bus accident too. The message I receive from all is that unless she wants help, she can't be forced. I explain again and again that I'm from out of state, that she isn't able to recognize how serious her situation is, that she is exhibiting delusional thinking and auditory hallucinations and seems to lack insight into her mental state, that she is so loved and missed, that I'm so worried for her safety. Legal guardianship is suggested, but the lawyers I contact explain sympathetically that it would likely take years and thousands of dollars to prove her incompetent by a California court, and that the process would very likely destroy our relationship with no guarantee that I would even be able to obtain guardianship in the end. I take the forms with me anyway. Maybe Shyloh would be willing to voluntarily let me take charge.

Back at her camp I try to explain how helpful trauma therapy could be, that I can help set it up, but she's reluctant and the thought of it makes her anxious. I ask her if she'd be willing to sign medical guardianship papers so that I can advocate for her legally and she tentatively agrees, but when I bring out the papers she changes her mind. I tell her if she agrees to come home with me I will trade in my rental for a bigger car and we'll drive back together, today, right now if she wants. She considers this, agrees to it one moment but ultimately won't commit. Finally I suggest we get her a post office box so she can send and receive letters and packages, money. She thinks this is a great idea and we walk up to the neighborhood post office about a half mile away and I am relieved to have found something that might help. But when we get there, she refuses to go in, paranoid of the cameras. Fighting back tears, I plead with the woman at the counter, explaining again and again that I'm from out of state, that I'll be going home soon, that the young woman talking to herself out front by the bushes is my daughter, that she has no address, no job, no ID to sign for a PO box, but I do have her birth certificate which I'd brought with me from home. The woman finally agrees to let me sign for Shyloh and tells me I can come back in the morning to get the key. Something, finally.

My flight is tomorrow. Shyloh keeps picking fights with me and I comply. I sense this is our way of dealing with the fact that I'm leaving soon, without her. We make it to the laundromat and she uses the few bills she's scrounged from recycling to get the two large garbage bags of clothes washed and dried, and buys herself a mixed drink in a can at the convenience store next door to drink while we wait. I don't understand why so much effort and her last few dollars are being put towards these discarded clothes that clearly don't fit her, when she needs so much and has so little. The whole situation stresses me out and I'm impatient and angry and struggle to sit there and watch while she folds them, as she argues now and then with the voices I can't hear. And then she proceeds to leave the clothes sitting in little piles along the window ledge, and I realize they weren't for her; they were meant for others in her "community," for any- one who happens by and needs them. And my confusion is washed with guilt for my own selfish impatience, and with a quiet pride for her beautiful generous heart.

I stop to see her the next morning on my way to the airport. She's "busy" doing nothing and barely acknowledges me at first. I give her the PO box number and the key, and a small stack of stamped envelopes with paper. I'd bought some nail polish in a pearly emerald green, a color I know she loves, and our last hour together she lets me paint her nails. Holding her hands in mine, I know in my heart that just being here as a witness to her life in this place has been important, for us both. With a long tearful hug and a promise to write, we say goodbye, and I head to the airport.

Shyloh and Raffie

Shyloh's creativity and courage, but also her declining mental state, will be reflected in the outdoor spaces she carves out for herself over the next couple years. None of these future homes will equal Fort Unicorn in imagination and ingenuity, but they will all be "home" to her nonetheless.

(poem written and shared with me in Fort Unicorn)
That's quite a racket
So you think you've arrived now?
Test your edge on a fingernail
Watch the slow sad death walk
Of a snail
Can you blame the adversary
Yes, but it just adds to the contrary

I feel heat in my cheeks
Flush from frustration
And quiet embarrassment
With a subtle pride
Tucked away inside
Cuz that racket you can't
Shut up about
Well it is my noise
Ripping holes thru your psyche
Giggling and tap dancing on conformity
There just aint a drop of norm left in me
Hater, thank yourselves
Your judgement is my creator - ACE

LETTERS TO FORT UNICORN
– JULY-AUG 2019

Dearest Shyloh,
July 14, 2019

I'm hoping you get this, because that means you went up and used the PO Box a la Fort Unicorn! =)

So much I want to say, but it feels like words get in the way. Do you know what I mean? I am so very thankful that I found you and that we were able to spend time together.

I went running yesterday. I tend to do a lot of my thinking when I run, and while going up a steep hill I was reflecting how I used to have the drive to push through anything. If it got hard, it would just make me push harder. I imagine that might've made me difficult to live with sometimes, when you and your brother were kids. I was thinking how I just don't have the same drive as I used to. Not sure if it's because I'm just tired and getting older, or if life has worn me down some. I guess I'm telling you this because I think I get it, what you were saying. I get that you're tired. I can understand the feeling of being so broken that you just can't imagine trying to put the pieces back together again. I still have that bear paw coffee mug you gave me. I loved that mug and I remember how bummed I was when I accidentally broke it. And how you collected all the pieces up and spent hours gluing it back together for me. It holds my colored pencils and pens, and even tho I can't use it for coffee anymore, I think I love it even more now. It's scarred and imperfect and reminds me of love and life.

Of course we won't ever be the same, our "whole" selves are gone, but we'll have a scarred beauty and new strengths and wisdom. So please don't give up, and I won't either.

I am so glad to have a picture in my mind of where you are, and I hope you're able to stay there safely as long as you need to. Please know and remember that I'm here for you, that I love you as you are!

Loving you always,
Your MAMABEAR

Dearest Shyloh,
July 21, 2019

I'm in Las Vegas right now, do you feel me nearby? =) I'm here with one of my boxers for a tournament. About the last 30 min or so of the flight coming into Vegas, the sky was so clear and it was the most spectacular view of the desert and the mountains. I couldn't help but wonder if you had seen that same view when you flew into Vegas a couple years ago? Hard to believe it's been that long already!!. And then getting off the plane, there were signs for Vegas weddings everywhere in the airport, and I wondered how that whole adventure was for you and Matt. You and I never really got a chance to talk about any of it, seems there's been one crisis after another since then... it all seems like forever ago.

I haven't heard from you for a while! Last text you sent said your phone was about to die, I'm wondering if you just haven't bothered to go charge it again yet? Or maybe it's lost, or stolen? Did you make it up to the post office yet? I hope you write me a letter soon! I can't force you to get help, or come home, but I at least want us to stay in contact, to know you're "ok" and safe.

I fly home in a couple hours. I didn't spend any time in downtown Vegas, but this morning I drove

out to Red Rock Canyon and went on a long run
in the mountains. It was gorgeous! I took pictures,
but you know how those are, they just can't capture
the magnitude of the landscape, so I deleted them.
It was so beautiful and grand and immense and
ancient, helped to make all of our troubles feel so
small and trivial. The boxer that I came out here
with won the Championship in his class. I'll be going
to San Jose in Sept to corner him for the World
Master's Championships. Probably a little too far to
drive down to see you in San Diego, but I would if
there's time, and if I know where to find you then.

I love you. I hope you are doing ok. Please send
me a letter, and call or text me! You are in my heart
and on my mind always...

Loving you fiercely, Mamabear

ps

Hi again! Wanted to add something before I
sent this out.

Heard from Miguel this morning (don't be mad
at him, I'm thankful that he contacted me!), he
said it looked like you'd packed up and left????
My heart sank, but I'm hoping you found a better
spot... maybe one with a waterfall like in your
dream? ;)

So now I'm again worried and anxious, as I can
no longer picture where you are or imagine that
you're ok and safe in Fort Unicorn. I'm wondering if

perhaps you went with that guy Sammy somewhere?
I liked him, he seemed like a good person though also
very troubled, but he seemed to care about you. I
hope if you're with him that he has your back. I hope
you still have your post office box key!

Love love love love you!! xoxoxoxoxo

Dearest Shyloh!!!!
July 30, 2019

Just got your letter today!!!!! =)) And I got
the birthday letter you sent for your brother too,
and I sent it on to his address.

I'm so glad you made it to the post office finally!
And now that I know there's a good chance you'll
get this, it makes writing to you so much more fun!
=)

Sorry you lost Fort Unicorn! But I know you and
also your creative home-making abilities... speaking
of home-making, I'll say it again (and again, and
again...), if you ever decide you're tired of the life
you're living, and you want to come back home, I
will do whatever I can to help make it happen.

Hoping your phone is just dead and not lost or
stolen... it's time for me to put more minutes on it
if you still have it.

I'm so so glad to hear from you!!! =))

I just added that song you sang me to my playlist. Sometimes I just listen to it on a loop while I'm running and picture us in your tent, you leaning back into your camp chair with eyes closed, singing it softly. I wish I'd recorded you... you still have such a beautiful voice. It carries so much emotion and soul. I always loved listening to you sing! So many songs remind me of you, and us. Remember all those duets we'd sing in the car? =)

I was able to sell all your wire wrapped pendants that I brought back with me, got about $200 for you! I can send it to you as a debit card once we agree on a pin# you'll remember, so I can have it activated for you before I send it.

Ok, getting ready to go to the gym. I'll write more later. I love you!!!!!!!!! xoxox

Buongiorno Principessa!!

It's Sun am, a beautiful day. It rained pretty good last night and everything feels cool and fresh and clean. Of course, I just watered the veggie garden too. Seems like the best way to get it to rain is to water the garden! Haha

I extracted honey from the hives yesterday too. I think you'd love it! I invested in a couple real bee suits which made the whole thing much less stressful. Wish there was a way I could get some honey to you... maybe I can send a jar to your PO box?

I'm including a stamped envelope with this letter and some paper to write on, as it appeared your envelopes may have gotten wet? I'm really hoping you're doing ok, and love love love hearing from you. Please tell me about your new spot so I can picture you somewhere in my mind, it eases the missing and worrying.

You are on my mind and in my heart constantly. When you decide you're ready, I can be there within a few days to help you come home. Please remember that you are loved and missed!!! Loving you always, Mamabear

Dearest Shyloh!
Aug 11, 2019

Well, I'm going to continue on with the assumption that you're getting my letters and that I'll be getting one from you any day now. ;) Hoping that you're getting my letters anyway. And so, I will keep writing until I hear otherwise.

I'm off to the gym, just wanted to get a letter

started to you. I write a little each day and then send it out Monday morning. I'm hoping you're doing ok. I wish there was a way to reach you, I feel like if I could just be close by, if we could just talk every day, it would help both of us. I'm glad for your friend Miguel, who lets me know if you're ok and safe. He's a good friend to you in that sense, and he seems to care about you, even if he says you can be kind of mean to him. Don't need to tell him I told you that tho ;) Ok, back later! Xoxoxo

Hello again.

Well, it's been about 2 weeks now since I received your letter. Haven't heard anything else from you which makes me sad. I check in with Miguel about once a week to see if he's seen you and to ask if you're doing ok. So far he says you are, though he says you seem pretty irritated with him when he visits. I obviously don't know him, and don't know your relationship with him, but from my perspective I am very thankful for him, he's been a friend by giving me a way to at least know if you're alive and where to find you. Without that I feel such a hole in my heart.

******

I heard from Miguel this morning that you're gone again and he doesn't know where you are ... =(sigh

I know that that's part of the life you've chosen, and that you can't necessarily stay in one spot if you're not paying rent (I'm hoping we can find a way to get you an apartment or something once your settlement is done), but it just tears me up to not know if you're ok. Don't even know if you're getting my letters.

I still have that $200 from selling your wire-wrapped rocks. I'd be glad to get you another phone and send you some cash. I just need to know that you're checking your box...

It's Sunday and I'll be sending this out first thing in the morning. I plan to call the lawyer about your Greyhound case tomorrow and if I hear anything I'll write it in my next letter. He's said he thought we should be hearing something soon about the settlement. No matter what the final amount ends up being, it will definitely help make your situation a little easier.

You asked me when I was there if I had any regrets... I only truly have one. I wish I could relive your and your brother's childhoods. I would laugh and play with you more, hug you tighter, would cherish every moment. I wish I knew then that I was going to lose you like this someday,

I would've held on harder. Who knew, I never would've imagined this.

I suppose I'll end this letter. Honestly, I'm losing hope that you're even getting them. It would help so much if you would just borrow someone's phone and call me.

I miss you, Shyloh. Whether you believe you need help or not doesn't have to be the issue. It could instead be, aren't you getting tired of this? Of being dirty and hungry, and always having to watch your back, of having your few special belongings stolen all the time, to scramble to keep a place to sleep. To find water. To stay safe. Tired of the lows that come from the not-so-high highs. Of being lonely and scared. Please consider coming home for a bit, you don't have to stay. Just long enough to get your head straight, to get some resources in place, to put together a sustainable plan. Please remember, when you're ready for a change, Shyloh, there is help for you to make it happen. I know, you're probably sick of hearing me say that.

Loving and missing you,
Mamabear

CASTLE OF GRACE
– DECEMBER 27, 2019

I stop writing letters once the post office sends my last several back unclaimed. Then Shyloh starts calling again, usually from a stranger's borrowed phone, or from a store, sometimes from the trolley station's pay phone.

Shyloh asks when I can come back to visit, and part of me wants to drop everything and go immediately. I'll be taking my elite female boxer to compete in the 2020 Olympic Trials in Louisiana just before Christmas and I'm committed to helping her train in preparation, but I assure Shyloh I'll see her for New Year's.

Sometimes when she calls she asks if I can send money, $100 so she can get a motel room for a night, or $50 to buy some food or clothes, and I go round and round in my head struggling with these requests. Am I enabling her addiction by giving her money? I know some would say yes, but it's more complicated than that. I'm torn by the knowledge that her existence is so hard, and the likelihood that rational decision-making may be nearly impossible for her much of the time. Withholding money to make a statement that I'm opposed to her choices won't force her to "hit bottom"; instead, it only assures that she won't be able to take the occasional hot bath, or eat a fresh meal not dug from a dumpster, that she may be forced to do things I don't want to imagine to merely survive. So, I decide to send her money when I can. Because she doesn't have an ID, I can't wire it directly to her, but from time to time she'll meet someone she trusts who has an ID and I send money to her in their name. Coordinating this is often a challenge. She tells me she'd moved from Fort Unicorn to a spot near the post office for a while but is now in Ocean Beach. She is usually cryptic when I ask for details about her day to day life, still paranoid of the airways, but is thrilled that I'll be coming to see her soon.

She calls several times over the weeks before my visit to confirm over and over that she has the day and time of arrival correct and I can tell she's very excited, as am I. She assures me she will be at the airport to meet me when I land, and though I love the idea, I'm skeptical, and press her for an address or landmark where we can plan to meet just in case. She's reluctant, but finally shares with me the general location of where she's been staying, tells me it's under Interstate-8 near the trolley depot. She calls her new spot The Castle.

I get off the plane and head towards the stairs that lead to the rental car shuttle. Shyloh and I used to joke about greeting each other at the airport with a sign like you see in the movies, and as I head down the stairs I scan the people waiting there, some holding up signs with names, half expecting and hoping to see her. I don't.

Waiting in line for the shuttle outside I continue to crane my neck looking for her, and then it's my turn to board. I'm not terribly surprised, but I am disappointed. She'd been so insistent that she'd be here to meet me. Thankfully I do have a vague idea of where to find her, so as the shuttle bounces along towards the rental car lot, I pull up the road she'd given me on my phone, marked on my GPS as The Castle, about ten miles away.

I'm pulling out of the parking lot with my rental when my phone rings. The airport attendant informs me that my daughter is there waiting for me and I ask the attendant to please let Shyloh know I'll be there in ten minutes, to wait for me in front of the terminal, and I make a U-turn to head back to the airport.

I see her, sitting on the curb, as I'm steering around the line of taxis. She's holding up her skateboard and waving it back and forth like a sign, MOM spray-painted on the underside in bright white paint and my heart leaps with joy and I smile at our private joke as I jump out to hug her, momentarily blocking the traffic behind me. She's lean and tan, dressed like a skater but with her own stylish flair. She's wearing a backwards baseball cap and has recently been shaving one side of her head, but the shoulder length hair from the other side peeks out in colorful dyed oranges and reds. Even living as she does, she's beautiful, managing to hold on to her whimsical sense of fashion. She jumps in the car with her small backpack and board and hands me a large bouquet of flowers. They're slightly wilted and look as though they may have been pulled from the trash, but I absolutely love them and tell her so. And I love them especially because of the effort that I know went into getting them to me today.

As we head to my airbnb we fall into comfortable, familiar chatter, but both of us are impatient with the inadequacy of words. Over the previous weeks Shyloh and I had been talking again about her coming home, even if just for a visit. Because she doesn't have an ID, flying back isn't an option, and getting a new ID is too big an obstacle for her at this point, but I tell her I'm prepared to rent an SUV and we can drive back together, and she's finally agreed. I'm anxious to discuss and make plans for our return trip together but when I bring it up she informs me she doesn't plan to ever stop using, and that she only wants to go back for a day to visit her dad and brother and then I need to drive her back "home," that she lives here now. I balk at this; I thought she was ready to make a change? I tell her we can't drive three days and then turn right around and drive back. I'm too caught up in the details and in "get things done" mode; should I humor the idea no matter how impractical if it will get her home?

We drop off my bag and put my flowers in a glass of water, and since she'll be staying with me at the airbnb, head to The Castle to get her things. I park near the trolley depot, and we begin walking, and though I don't know what to expect as she leads me down the empty sidewalk towards her current home, I can't help envisioning Fort Unicorn, the only real context I have for her existence here at this point. There are no buildings or people around, only the concrete of the road we're walking along and sturdy girders supporting the several expressways rumbling with traffic overhead. We climb the rubble under one of the girders, and near the top of the rocky embankment I see the shadow of a small "wall" about twenty inches high, maybe eight feet long, built from stacked riprap and gravel... her Castle wall?

We're at the top now and must bend over to not bump our heads on the concrete above us; the steady roar above is deafening. It's dark up here, even mid-day. On the other side of the miniature wall, I can make out a depression dug into the riprap, into the gravel and dirt, roughly ten inches deep, lined with a large fuzzy blanket, just big enough for a body to curl up in. Small plastic totes with a few toiletries and craft supplies sit on the blanket, a couple battered suitcases and several garbage bags around the perimeter. I've got a lump in my throat, picturing my child sleeping alone in this hole and I want to cry out, but I instead comment on the little parasol with the pretty oriental design that she's braced against the stones near her bed, and the empty soda bottle sitting atop the wall with the small bouquet of colorful plastic flowers. She digs out a sketch pad from under the blanket and grabs one of the suitcases, and I struggle to push the image from my mind as we head back to the car.

We detour on our way back to the airbnb so she can show me her evening route of dumpster diving, the flower shop she passes nightly and its dumpster where she lovingly salvaged my bouquet last night. She asks if I'd join her on a nighttime excursion. I consider it.

We stop by the grocery store, and I tell her to grab whatever she wants and for a while she's like a child bouncing from aisle to aisle, excitedly putting items in the basket until the strain of decision-making starts to take its toll on her. At checkout I know there's way too much food here for two but I buy it all anyway, desperate to do anything that might bring us both some comfort.

Once back to the apartment, it's obvious that the day's events have already exhausted both of us. As I unpack and put away the food, Shyloh takes a long hot shower. For nearly two hours I hear the water running and her alternately singing, sobbing and arguing loudly to herself.

Our first day together, as with my last visit, is emotionally exhausting but mostly pleasant. Her temperament has been almost childlike today, but I relish the rare opportunity to pamper her. At one point I ask her what the three hardest things are about the life she is living and she answers without pause, in this order: *hot water; shame; existing.*

We barely eat any of the food that night, but instead cuddle on the couch and I gently massage skin cream into the painful cracks and calluses on her swollen hands and feet. I make up the pull-out bed for her but she ultimately opts for the simple couch. And when I hear her crying out in her sleep, I lie with her until the nightmare finally lets go and she drifts off again.

Over the next several days I witness what I imagine are

the fractured parts of her mind in battle for her attention, presenting almost as three separate people, and our conversations are at times erratic and impossible to follow. She asks me cautiously what I think of the name Grace, derived from her street name Ace; what if she decided to change her name? I say I think it's pretty but that I like Shyloh better, and she promises that of course she will always be *Shyloh* to me, that I'm her mama. She says she wants to play dress-up, and proceeds to pull out the clothes she's brought and, giggling, puts them on in various combinations, makes up her hair and face, takes another two-hour shower. One of her outfits includes a pair of billowy genie pants in a muted patchwork that she'd found in a dumpster, and I comment on how beautiful they are, still amazed at what people will throw away. I try to play along but it's forced and clumsy and inwardly I'm panicking a little. She reverts to almost childlike speech and sings to herself while she doodles in her sketchbook. Then without provocation she suddenly snarls angrily at me, and when I reply, startled and confused, I realize she's not talking to me but to the voices that seem to torment her constantly. And then taking on a hard streetwise persona, she declares that Shyloh was a weak bitch, that she had to be killed, that her name is now Grace.

Surreal is the word that keeps coming to me. The definition: *something that's a bizarre mix of elements, often jarring*

and seemingly nonsensical. Yes, the word describes this, my emotions, all of this, perfectly. It's all so surreal to witness and exhausting to process, and because she's staying with me and I'm afraid to leave her in the apartment alone, I have no immediate respite. When she does step out for several hours at a time I drive to a nearby nature reserve and run the trails, music blasting in my headphones, pushing hard up the steep hills until the ache in my legs and lungs temporarily mutes the ache in my heart.

Except for that first night she doesn't sleep with me at the apartment, leaving early evening and then showing up late morning the next day to nap and eat. She brings back several large garbage bags over the next few days and proceeds to spread the contents out on the living room floor as if sorting through them and I rebuke myself constantly for my trivial concern over the cleanliness of the airbnb carpet that keeps pushing forefront in my mind. Most of what she's brought truly does seem like garbage and I don't understand why it's here, but there are a few useful items too. I complained out loud at one point yesterday that I'd forgotten my toothpaste and she now hands me a partial tube salvaged from a dumpster last night. I awkwardly thank her but reply that I'll buy a new one, and immediately regret my thoughtless refusal and all it implies. I should've accepted her humble gift, whether I meant to use it or not, recognizing too late how degrading my constant push to help her without allowing her to reciprocate must feel. I vow to pay attention to and accept her gestures in the future.

I'd come to San Diego with an agenda to bring her home. But soon the realization hits me that I'm not sure it's even feasible for me to get her home safely by myself; her behavior is too unpredictable, her thinking too erratic, and she readily admits that she's been actively using meth, and synthetic opioids which she refers to as *research chemicals*. I'm concerned what detox on the road would look like and keep envisioning her running off in the middle of nowhere and having no way of finding her. So, I'm struggling with how to accept the idea that I may be leaving her here again.

I'll be leaving tomorrow, heading home again without her. She says she doesn't want to leave, and at the same time she says she does. Neither of us knows how to reconcile this, and we spend the day arguing about trivial things. She is sitting with her legs spread out in front of her on the living room floor amongst the items she'd strewn there throughout the week. I've tried several times to straighten up the mess and throw away the obvious pieces of garbage – the wrappers, crumpled paper, broken pens – but she savagely protects it.

"Get your fucking hands off that! Don't fucking touch my stuff!" I've been prodding her gently all day to start packing up her things, explaining over and over that if she's not going back with me I will need to leave on the plane early in the morning and we have to clean this up. I'm getting frustrated and angry, but my mind is only on the task at hand, not on

what lies beyond that. It's dark when she finally gets her suitcase packed and we decide to get food at the Chinese restaurant down the block, the only place open on New Year's Eve.

We're both solemn as we sit in the car with our takeout
dinner at the top of a hill and watch fireworks in the distance.
I play Bonnie Raitt singing "Angel from Montgomery," one
of our favorites, on my phone, and we sing along while tears
roll down both our faces. Neither of us is prepared for what
must come next.

I park at the edge of the empty road in front of her under-
pass, and we sit there in the dark for a while saying nothing.
It's after midnight. I'll be heading to the airport in a few hours
and still have to clean the apartment and pack. I knew intel-
lectually that this moment would come but there are no words
to describe how impossible it feels. Finally I tell her it's time
to go but she won't get out of the car. I ask, plead again, *are
you coming home with me?* She again says no. Then you need
to get out of the car. I start to cry, sob, I'm yelling now, you
need to get out of the car, I have to leave. We're both sobbing now and finally I get out and take her suitcases and bags
out of the car and set them on the sidewalk as she screams at
me not to touch her stuff. She gets out of the car and angrily
starts carrying her bags across the street, and screams over
her shoulder, "Just fucking leave!"

I'm shaking, sobbing. I can barely see the road through
my tears as I drive back towards the airbnb, overwhelmed
with guilt and an agonizing sorrow. I'm almost back to the
apartment when I turn around and go back to where I'd left

her. I feel my way up the rocks, and using my phone's light, I find her curled on the blanket. I lie down against her back and wrap myself around her, hugging her to me. I love you, I love you, I'm so sorry, and she whispers, "It's okay, Mama. I made my choice. I love you too." We lie like this for what feels like a lifetime, and then I get to my feet.

As I'm cleaning up the apartment I come across a large plastic bag that Shyloh has left behind. Opening it I find multiple small packages bound in used wrapping paper and ribbons. There's a note attached, "Ho ho ho, Merry Xmas!- I didn't put names on them, but you can decide who should get what ;)- xoxoxo"

Each small gift has undoubtedly been rescued from some dumpster: a handsome men's watch, likely for her brother; a pretty woman's coin purse that I think my mom, her grandma, would love; a small dragonfly wind chime. And in one, carefully wrapped in delicate purple tissue paper, are the genie pants. I call them my "Shyloh pants" and hold her in my heart every time I wear them.

SOLUTIONS – JANUARY 2020

It takes weeks to decompress once I return home. To think of her, to remember her at all, means to ache for her. How to hold Shyloh close to my heart, without being swallowed by the intense and constant sorrow? I seek out a grief and trauma counselor for myself, and over the next couple months she guides me in finding tools that will help carry me forward: *compassion, letting go, acceptance, forgiveness*. Learning to be more compassionate in the moment, not defaulting to problem-solving. Learning to let go, letting go of the past, letting go of what could have been, of what I wish could be. Acceptance of what is, and forgiving myself for my faults and weaknesses.

Shyloh calls me from jail one afternoon a couple weeks after I return home and tells me she's been arrested for sleeping on the beach. She tells me the officers were exceptionally rude in waking her, and unnecessarily rough in putting her in the patrol car, and she's understandably angry. I can feel her frustration and it makes me angry too. While I recognize there are laws about sleeping in public places, and these laws need to be enforced to some extent, it seems so ridiculously futile to arrest, charge, and fine someone who has literally nothing and is just struggling to exist in a place. And now too, her few belongings that were left behind on the beach will undoubtedly be absorbed by the community of people who live out there with her. She asks me to pay the $5000 bond that will allow her to be released before her arraignment, but knowing she almost certainly won't show back up for court, I tell her I'm sorry, no. She hangs up furiously, but not before spitting a few venomous words at me through the phone. When she's arraigned and released a week later, she calls again from a borrowed phone to apologize. It's okay, I say, I understand. I tell her I love her.

IHOT – MARCH 2020

I am still wracking my brain for a solution for how to get resources to Shyloh and imagine a program that sends social workers out onto the streets to find and help the people there who are unable or unwilling to access resources on their own. Turns out there really is such a program in San Diego. It's called IHOT, In-Home-Outreach-Team, and after calling I discover that Shyloh fits all the criteria for eligibility: *18 years and older, residing in San Diego County (family may live out of region); has serious mental health symptoms that contribute to functional impairment in activities of daily living, social relations and/or ability to sustain housing; declines mental health services, may have sporadic contact with an outpatient mental health program, but has discontinued recommended treatment; has had one, or more, of the following events in the past year: Psychiatric hospitalization, Psychiatric Emergency Room visit, Police/PERT involvement, Incarceration.*

During the long intake interview I describe my daughter, how talented and loved and terribly missed Shyloh is. I describe her chronic addictions, family history of mental illness, her rapid decline after the bus accident, her paranoia and desperate living situation, her stints in jail and the psych hospital, and her insistent refusal to seek help. Josh is assigned as her outreach worker and, acting as intermediary the next time Shyloh calls, I manage to arrange for her to meet Josh at a predetermined spot.

Shyloh calls me that afternoon from the new phone Josh has brought her, and for the next month she stays in touch with me regularly, sends me poems and photos of the sketches and crafts she's working on. She tells me excitedly that I've got a birthday package on the way, that Josh has helped her with postage. But when I ask her if she's meeting with him regularly, and how it's going, she's evasive and implies that she doesn't trust him. I try contacting Josh myself to ask if something happened and I'm told that because he has already made initial contact, privacy laws prevent him from talking to me. And a week later I'm told she's been dropped from the program because she was uncooperative. I'm baffled and frustrated; wasn't that why we needed their services in the first place??

I wake to find a text message from Shyloh. It's a poem she'd sent at about 1:00 AM:

Another lucid living lovely
Lacking only everything that mattered yesterday.
Even this day spins so far
Away from its point, it's a wander - Grace

When I receive the birthday package I am overcome with love and gratitude wrapped tightly in sorrow. There's a long rambling letter that makes me laugh through my tears, and a whimsical birthday card. She's made me a miniature bonsai of twisted copper wire, rooted on a small stone, a "tree of life" with tiny chunks of turquoise and little bits of mother of pearl woven into the ends of each copper branch. And wrapped carefully in a plastic bread bag is a tiny plant, a succulent, potted tenderly into the spiral hollow of a seashell. I'm amazed this delicate living thing has survived the journey, and marvel at the resilience of life.

A SMALL FORTUNE – JUNE 2020

It's been nearly three years since the bus accident, and after several ridiculously low offers, Greyhound has finally agreed to a settlement of $100,000. I think this is still too low. Our lawyer tells me we probably could have gotten at least double the amount if Shyloh had been more involved, had been dependably reachable and clear headed. Still, even after his 25%, it's a solid chunk of change for her. My dilemma is how to manage the money, a more difficult task than I would've imagined, both logistically and philosophically.

Shyloh left a wake of credit card debt and unpaid bills when she moved to San Diego. I'm concerned that creditors might come after the money so I create an account for it in my name. This isn't the first time I've had to do this. Years ago after Shyloh injured her knee while hiking with the teen wilderness program, she won a $10,000 worker's comp settlement. She asked me then to serve as her power of attorney, confessing that she didn't trust herself with that amount of money, that she wanted me to manage it for her, that she trusted me and knew I had her best interests always at heart. That happened during one of her periods of "recovery." We paid off long overdue fines, replaced her library card, found her a place to live, bought a bus pass, renewed her driver's license. And then she relapsed and called almost daily with a barrage of insults and accusations that it was her money, who the fuck did I think I was, give her her damn money. She was so incredibly nasty and persistent, I finally gave up and handed over a cashier's check for the remainder, roughly $7000. Not surprisingly, the money was gone in a week. This settlement is substantially more. Am I prepared for that sort of attack again?

I'm trying to calculate how we can stretch her money for as long as possible, but what does that mean for someone with almost nothing, someone who needs so much, for someone living on the streets, refusing any conventional assistance, refusing to stop using drugs, refusing psychological help? Should I think big picture, hold on to the money and wait until she's "ready" as an incentive to get real help? She'd then have the financial resources to get and stay on her feet, at least for a while. This amount of money could easily help to support her for several years. I run a quick search for apartments in San Diego, but the rents are too high and logistically I'm not sure how that would work with me living out of state. I search apartments for rent in my own neighborhood and find two for a little over $800 a month and envision her living right down the street, stopping over for coffees in the mornings. We would go for walks, work together in the garden, she could go back to school, get a job, get back into counseling, back on medications. I have to stop myself. What if she's never ready? It may just be that THIS is the reality of my daughter's life and so also the reality of mine as her mother. Maybe there is no balm to make this easier, no solution. I struggle with this kind of acceptance. It feels like giving up to me. I've always been able to accomplish whatever I put my mind to and that perseverance drives me still.

I talk to James, close friends, my mother, searching for answers to how I should manage this money. They all patiently listen and offer words of support, but none have real answers.

I consider then that a few dollars in her pocket day-to-day would surely help ease her daily struggles, even if it's barely a band-aid and may just prolong what feels like an inevitable, tragic end. How much money does one need per day to survive on the streets? I punch the settlement total into my calculator over and over in countless variations:

> One meal/day; bottled water:
> $TOTAL ÷ [$/day x 365] = 20.5 years
> What about toiletries, tampons, clothes?
> $TOTAL ÷ [$/week x 52] = 14 years
> What about the occasional hotel room to shower and rest?
> A phone, minutes, a used bike, a blanket?
> $TOTAL ÷ [$/month x 12] = 6.25 years
> San Diego is so expensive, and ironically the poorer you are the more expensive everything is.
> Maybe a storage unit? A small apartment?
> $TOTAL ÷ [$$/month x 12] = 2.5 years

My mind keeps getting stuck. Who am I to decide what she should spend her money on, what her necessities are, what "luxuries" she should allow herself, what life she should live? Maybe my opinion, my hopes, my heartbreak, my grief, have nothing to do with it.

The next time she calls I tell her Greyhound has settled and I'll have her check soon. I tell her I've found a couple very affordable apartments right near me and suggest that with the money she could come home and get her feet under her, that I'd be right down the street to help with whatever she might need. She quickly opposes the idea of an apartment, tosses out instead a request for a motorcycle, or maybe some vending machines. Our conversation is all over the place, and turns into ranting that I'm keeping her money from her, that I need to fly out there immediately and bring it to her, that she intends to bury it on the beach somewhere so it'll be safe.

"Bring it to me now, or I'll sue you!" I need to hold the phone away from my ear, reluctant to hang up but unable to stand the tirade. I'm finally able to get a word in and ask where she is. She refuses to tell me, paranoid of disclosing her location over the phone, saying instead, "Just come to California, ask around, everybody knows me!"

And then she disappears again. I file another missing person report. I have a list of numbers here on my desk, all the San Diego hospitals, multiple police departments, San Diego County sheriff, the morgue, and I call these numbers weekly, assured by all that if her body were found I'd be contacted. How unreal that this is my only comfort from the worry of not knowing. While I wait for her to show up again, I optimistically continue searching for solutions.

Journal entry: Sometimes I feel as though I'm wearing blinders, forcing my focus on only the activities directly ahead, a looming darkness threatening to swallow me. My heart is pounding constantly as if in *fight or flight* mode. I've never been inclined towards flight, but when I actually was fighting years ago, doing my walk-out to the boxing ring in front of a 2000+ crowd, climbing between the ropes to face whoever opposed me, my adrenaline would be controlled, spotlight focused and ready for battle. This feeling I have now is more like a constant, uncontrolled adrenaline dump. It's getting harder and harder to stay focused and takes so much energy just to function. I keep injuring myself through carelessness. I imagine this is a physical manifestation of my struggle to focus.

I feel so broken. When I talk to James about it, he replies with, "I'm sorry... I love you." What else really is there to say?

FAMZOO

I've found an online service called *FamZoo*, set up for parents to help their children learn to manage money. The *parent* debit card is linked to a bank account and preloaded, and money can be dispersed from the parent card to the child's card in real time. I would be able to see how and when the money is spent, I could lock the card if it's lost, and load the card whenever she needs money, but she wouldn't have access to the actual bank account. It's exactly the solution I've been searching for. Now I need to find her.

When she calls again three months later, I stress how much I worry when I don't hear from her. She apologizes, reminding me how hard it is to find a phone. But then she confesses tentatively that when she does find one she doesn't know how to decide who to call first: me, her dad, her brother, Grandma, an old friend. She doesn't say it directly, but it's clear to me that her voices criticize and berate her, implying that who she chooses to call first is somehow intensely significant. And because she can't decide, she often calls no one.

"I'm sorry. I love you," I say.

I explain about FamZoo, and though she's adamant that she won't ever use the debit card, that "they'll" be able to track her, that she doesn't want to become part of "the machine," I make plans to fly out and bring her the card anyway.

In the meantime, we also discover that Western Union allows small sum transfers using a security question, and by answering the question and providing the transfer number a person can receive the cash without an ID. I need to set these up in person with an actual Western Union agent rather than online or at a kiosk, which turns out to be a pain in the ass, especially with so many in-person transactions being limited due to COVID restrictions. Shyloh and I "agree" on $50 per week to be available every Tuesday. Thankfully I'm able to set up three $50 transfers at a time so I can have them ready for her in advance when she calls from her grocery store's Western Union desk, rarely on Tuesdays and often several days in a row rather than weekly. Sometimes she asks for $100 or $200 instead, explaining some urgent need, or that she's found someone with an ID who will sign for a hotel room for a few nights. I balk at these too frequent requests for more, fretting that she'll run out of money too soon. I wish someone could just tell me what to do. I search my soul constantly trying to untangle my worries. I can't ensure where the money will actually go, can't know whether I'm enabling her addictions, whether she'll lose it or get robbed, and I consider too that the money is hers after all. But when she does call from a hotel room a day or two later, showered and comfortable for the night under a roof, warm and safe behind a locked door, my heart rests easier that night too.

I recognize that some of the money is likely going to alcohol and drugs, but also that she can eat regularly, stop at Goodwill and replace clothes if needed, pick up necessities at the corner store, that this is helping to relieve some of the shame that I know torments her, and I can hear a subtle change in her voice, slightly less desperate. It doesn't ease the heartache of knowing how precarious her living situation is, but hearing her voice so often and knowing she is alive makes a world of difference in easing my mind.

Her periodic rants are terribly distressing, but she isn't always ranting when she calls. She often calls to just say hi, and we chat, describe our day's activities, or the weather, or reminisce about things that make us both smile. In nearly all of our phone conversations, at some point she pauses and begs me tearfully to come be with her. "Please, Mama, I need you. I need you more than they do." Oh, how that tugs at my heart.

I'm flying out next month to see Shyloh, and to bring her the debit card. I think back to when Shyloh lived nearby, how she and I loved to peruse secondhand stores and yard sales together to find each other treasures, the perfect shirt or shoes or book. We went for walks to nowhere in particular, or hung out for afternoons of crafting and watching movies, sobbing together at the sad parts, and losing ourselves to fits of uncontrolled giggling at nothing at all. An easy phone call away to talk each day about our lives and plans, dissecting each other's dreams. It's impossible to give up on the hope of her getting healthy someday and being present in my life again in a way that feels normal. I can't, won't let go of this hope, but for now I will immerse my heart into the sorrow and struggle of her life as it is.

A BROKEN HEART
– OCTOBER 20, 2020

I am about to have a minor surgery on my hand to address an old injury. During pre-op the surgeon discovers that my heart is in an irregular rhythm called *atrial fibrillation*, also known as AFib. I recall from Anatomy and Physiology class that the heart is made up of four chambers, a left and right atrium, and a left and right ventricle. The atria are the two chambers that collect deoxygenated blood from the body (right atrium) and oxygenated blood from the lungs (left atrium) and then push this blood into the ventricles which propel it forcefully into either the lungs (right ventricle) or the body (left ventricle). Atrial fibrillation occurs when the electrical signals controlling the contractions go haywire and instead of the rhythmic lub-Dub, lub-Dub, the "lub" becomes rapid and irregular and the atria are unable to efficiently refill the ventricles. I was also experiencing an *atrial flutter*, in which the "lub" becomes an ineffectual quiver. Though not necessarily immediately life-threatening conditions, there is a real risk of stagnating blood in the atria clotting and coming loose to cause a stroke. I am advised to make an appointment as soon as possible with my primary physician.

Over the past several months I often struggled to finish my four-mile runs, would have to walk up the hills I usually sprinted. I assumed this and the constant "fight or flight" racing and pounding in my chest, the exhaustion and insomnia and constant feelings of anxiety I've been experiencing over the past year were due to stress alone. This diagnosis helps to explain these perturbing symptoms; my heart is quite literally broken.

I delve into researching the condition and learn that atrial fibrillation is not an uncommon heart problem, but is usually found in an older, sedentary population, or those struggling with diabetes or obesity. I am none of these, but chronic stress can also bring it on. My primary care doctor puts me on heart medication, but it makes me feel like I'm stuck in mud, moving in slow motion, and I can't tolerate this. The doctor concedes that I can take the medication as needed instead of daily, but I choose not to take it at all. I consider Shyloh and her resistance to psychiatric medications, her similar complaint about how the meds made her feel.

I seek out a heart surgeon experienced in dealing with elite athletes, and she is confident that because we have caught this early I will be a perfect candidate for an *ablation*. In this procedure the areas of the heart that are creating the errant electrical signals and resulting erratic heartbeats are carefully identified and deadened through cauterization. The thought of this procedure is terrifying, but I'm hopeful to soon have relief from the constant erratic pounding in my chest and the intense feelings of anxiety it provokes.

I will need to be on a blood thinner for several weeks before we can do the procedure to ensure that any clots that may have already formed are dissolved. In the meantime, I book my flight to San Diego.

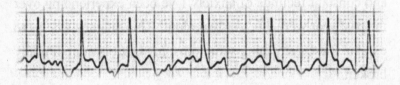

GOALS – NOVEMBER 21, 2020

I fly out in a few days but still don't know where to find her when I get there. When she calls I remind her that I'll be there soon and eventually we agree to meet at McDonald's and she gives me a street name. Her spot, she says, is nearby. She tells me she's been "adulting," her word for trying to act responsibly, and wants to discuss responsible ways to spend her money. This feels encouraging, but she bounces from reasonable, coherent ideas to outrageous ones, and I struggle to keep up, to know how to respond to the ones that make no sense. Her more reasonable goals are:

• to have a place 1x or 2x/week to take a hot bath

• to have a power source (she suggests a generator), specifically for the small wood burning tool she's found and is excited to try out

• to have somewhere safe to lock up important things "like receipts," so she can keep track of her spending, she says, like maybe a bank safety deposit box

I comment that this sounds a lot like an apartment and ask again if she'd consider letting me help her find one.

"No," she says; she likes being outside, she "likes the struggle." I wonder if it's not so much the struggle she likes but the fact that her life has been so utterly simplified, that there are no expectations of her other than surviving day to day, moment to moment. Another of her arguments is that she doesn't want to get accustomed to comfort, that it won't last, that she's finally gotten used to sleeping on the hard ground. What I believe she really means is that she's lost everything and everyone that has mattered to her too many times, has found herself at the bottom and climbed back out over and over, only to fall again and again. . . that it's just too hard to remember all that loss.

I fly out tomorrow. I am impatient to see her and hold her close but I'm also anxious about the upcoming visit. I decide to put to paper the issues that are weighing most heavily:

• The $$ - I'm torn by what I consider *her best interest* and what she argues is *her right, her money*. How much is enough, how much is reasonable? How much is safe? Her mental state and addictions cause her to be compulsive, impulsive, immature, unrealistic, short sighted. So it's my job as her power of attorney (as her mother?) to make those decisions, but do I manage it for her as she is, or as I would for myself?

• Her argument is that life is short, that she might die tomorrow, that every day is such a major struggle, that it's her money, that she earned it by the trauma she's endured ("having a bus fall on my head" is how she put it), so why shouldn't she be able to spend it how she wants? They are good arguments in many ways and push all my buttons.

• I need to keep replaying and practicing likely scenarios to help me manage the chaos when it happens, because in the moment I can easily get swept up in the emotion and irrationality of it all.

• I don't know how to get her to a hospital, but she needs to be treated for the several physical issues that have been troubling her lately, if not for a psych eval then at least antibiotics for the chronic bladder infections. She's convinced lately that hospitals are euthanizing the homeless.

• She says she doesn't want the debit card because *They* will be able to track her, but she wants the money and I need an efficient way to get it to her.

• Medication will likely calm the delusions and disorganized thinking and allow her to function more normally in society, but they will also likely dull her creativity, mute her passions, dampen the spark that makes Shyloh who she is. I really struggle with this one. Besides the fact that so far she won't agree to take them anyway, isn't it just caging her spirit to save it?

She asks me to help with unrealistic plans, but adamantly refuses the help that's actually needed. Or is it? Is her reality any less real to her than mine is to me? Are her choices really any less legitimate than mine? If she were to accept help and live the life I want for her, most likely medicated and possibly institutionalized, who is that actually best for? The life she is living, chosen or not, comes with these complications; that's the reality. And this is where I get sucked in over and over because I'm drawn to finding solutions, but I'm learning that some situations have no solutions. I recognize that the money may be enabling her addictions, but it's the mental illness, her inability to follow through, to reason clearly, that has her truly stuck. So instead I choose to view what I'm doing as enabling her existence as best I can. And, yes, when I know she's living, my life is better too.

A good friend shared a book of quotes, and the following really spoke to me:

> *I think the SEEKER'S PATH is about arriving at a place, a bottom, where WILL & EGO aren't big enough to serve the thing that you are after, which is TRUTH. So you have to give up trying to control things. You attend to them. The difference is major. The path is about a larger, more mysterious context, which makes things scarier and more confusing, but it all makes BEAUTY possible. Truth, like beauty, is not ultimately in your power, it is larger. – Tom Jay, sculptor*

> *Living is a form of not being sure, not knowing what next or how... the artist never entirely knows. We guess. We may be wrong, but we take LEAP after LEAP in the dark. – Agnes De Mille*

> *The spiritual path is about learning how to die. That involves not just death at the end of this*

*particular life, but all the falling apart that happens
continually. The fear of death – which is also the fear
of groundlessness, of insecurity, of not having it all together – seems to be the most fundamental thing that
we have to work with... we have so much fear of not
being in control, of not being able to hold onto things.
Yet the true nature of things is that you're never in
control. You're never in control. You can never hold
on to anything. That's the nature of how things are...
make your path about training to relax with groundlessness and the panic that accompanies it... train to
die continually. – Pema Chodron*

I find these quotes comforting. And I consider that
maybe Shyloh sees these truths innately. That it's me who
often doesn't see clearly.

A HOTEL ROOM – NOVEMBER 30, 2020

Friday

I pick up my rental car and drive from the airport to the McDonald's where I find an outdoor table to wait, but after about an hour I decide to explore the area and look for her. I see a man who's been sleeping along the side of the road, now rising to stretch. He eyes me suspiciously as I walk toward him, but Shyloh has assured me that the other unhoused folks living in her neighborhood know her, and so I ask if he knows Grace, and tell him that I'm her mom. The sentence sounds foreign to me, but I continue: Does he know where I could find her? He brightens, says I look like her, that he'll go check if she's home. He gestures for me to follow down the embankment.

We arrive at a series of tunnels, underpasses, along a bike trail, the concrete decorated with layers of colorful tags and graffiti. He calls her name into the shadows under one.

"Hey, Grace! This lady says she's your mom!!"

I see her silhouette coming toward us as she replies excitedly, "Hey, Mama!" and I'm filled with relief to have found her so easily. After we hug, she shows me around her space at the far end of the tunnel near the opening. I love that she's decorated everything, has put her personal artistic touches everywhere amidst the litter here; I love that glimpses of her spirit are visible in this place. She has a tent, torn and worthless against the elements but good enough to offer privacy, and proudly shows me her "lumpy but comfy" bed made up of a blanket laid over several layers of rubber bike tires. I consider how comfy I would find this arrangement. A couple other little camps are set up farther down in a darker part of the tunnel, but Shyloh has claimed this whole lighted end for herself, and I'm strangely comforted by this.

It is so good to see her. She gives me a t-shirt she's found and washed, with San Diego and the iconic California Republic bear on the front. I thank her and wonder aloud how she'd known I'd wanted one of these??

"Knew you'd like it, Mamabear," she says, smiling.

On this trip, I've planned – wrong word – *studied* how best to respond when our shared reality starts to fade and her voices take over. My intention, my mission, other than bringing her the debit card, is just to be with her, with "love, acceptance and curiosity" in my heart. We take a long walk as she shows me around her neighborhood, and although her voices keep intruding on our conversations, our first afternoon together feels light and easy. I believe this ease may have less to do with my studied intentions, though, and more to do with her being fairly tuned in today. She reminds me from time to time that her name is now Grace, but she does so tolerantly, and I don't really try very hard to remember. I think we're both struggling with letting Grace take Shyloh's place in my mind.

I had preloaded $250 on her debit card and am relieved that despite her earlier protestations she accepts it readily and uses it immediately at the 7-11 to purchase a black cherry lemonade Snapple, one of her "new favs." At one point as we walk, when she stops and cocks her head as if straining to hear and then mutters something to herself, I ask about the voices, what they're like. She candidly describes that at the moment they're like the steady quiet roar of spectators in the stands, as though they're watching and always judging her. If she stops and listens carefully, though, she can sometimes hear more clearly the constant, critical commentary. She quiets abruptly, as if reprimanded for sharing this, and changes the subject.

By nightfall her composure begins to unravel. A simple trip to the Dollar Store to get a toothbrush, and then an hour and $97 later we are in the parking lot of the strip mall with her Dollar Store loot spread out in my rental car trunk. I am trying to help her organize it, but she instead seems to revel in the experience of having all that stuff. Most of it probably had a purpose in her mind at some point but looking at it there and knowing what (in my mind anyway) she is truly in need of, I find it hard to understand the purchases.

Then she tells me enthusiastically that she's going to "quick jog over to TJ Maxx to get some socks, be right back!" I stay in the car to call and talk to James for a bit and attempt to settle my racing heart, but after an hour I start to worry and go looking for her.

I find her skipping around the store with a cart piled high with coats and clothes, various electronics, a giant umbrella, and other significantly less practical items. I try to explain to her that her card isn't a credit card, that there's only $150 left on it after the Dollar Store purchases, that we could find some of these things cheaper somewhere else. She becomes increasingly obstinate until finally I tell her I'll wait for her out front, deciding I'm going to just let this play out on its own. It's nearly 10 p.m., my heart is pounding and my mind is frazzled, I want to get some sleep. Another half hour goes by and I peer in through the glass doors and can see the security guard looking at me, then towards the cash registers and then back at me, a troubled expression on his face. Back inside I find Shyloh at the checkout arguing loudly with the manager that he's stolen her fucking money. She has obviously over-spent and has returned most of the stuff but because she's run her debit card as credit, the money can't be refunded immediately and she's not able to buy anything now, not even the socks she'd originally come in for. It is a little confusing, and the manager continues patiently trying to explain this – that her money will show back up on the card in a few days, but there is a zero balance on it now. Shyloh absolutely won't accept this and is getting increasingly animated, and as there seems to be no other solution and I'm worried the police will soon be called, I pay for the remaining items and we head back to the car. She is too agitated now for any conversation and I'm too exhausted, so when she refuses to come back to the airbnb with me I readily agree to drop her off near where I'd found her that afternoon and we plan to meet at McDonald's in the morning for breakfast.

I'm frazzled, but all in all, it felt like a pretty good day. I tried to approach the day with curiosity, and she shared a bit of her internal reality with me. She accepted the card, and though the spending had gotten out of hand, I feel as though I've accomplished something huge today. Back at my place I call James and recount the rest of the evening. I have a single glass of wine and fall into bed with a vague sensation of confidence that I'm prepared to handle whatever comes these next several days.

Saturday

Shyloh bought a little notebook planner during her Dollar Store spree the night before, and the next morning we sit at a table outside McDonald's while she eats her McGriddles and jots down her "adulting" goals and the activities she'd like us to do together while I'm in San Diego. We spend several hours doing this, and though I enjoy listening to the creative ideas she comes up with, I need to keep reminding myself to let this "planning" itself be our activity. Many of her goals are, not surprisingly, quite unrealistic, but some are very feasible. She stresses that she "really, really" wants to go for a drive together to Joshua Tree National Park; she's heard it is beautiful and wants us to go hiking there. I love the idea, and my mind begins to make the logical switch from vague planning to getting things done. This is my MO after all: determine goal; make it happen. The planning, though, quickly becomes exhaustingly frustrating for both of us. I'm again getting an up-close look at how her days run into each other, and nothing ultimately gets accomplished, how disordered thinking can make it nearly impossible to move from A to B to C. Saying she doesn't accomplish anything isn't entirely accurate; she does manage to "do" a great deal, but most of her doing isn't especially productive (I'm beginning to despise the word *productive* as much as I despise the word *potential*).

Later that afternoon she asks me to help her get a hotel room for the rest of my stay, and I agree. When the hotel attendant asks for her name and ID so she can have her own key, she tells him sternly that her name is Grace (no last name) and that since she's paying for the room, they must give her a key. The attendant looks at us both warily and explains that without an ID on file he won't be able to give her access to a room. I explain that she's my daughter, that I'll just let her use one of the two keys he's given me. Fine, he says, but she won't get a replacement key if she gets locked out. I reserve the room through Tuesday so I can make sure she gets checked out on time before I leave Wednesday morning. Shyloh suggests that I stay in the room with her, but I decline. As much as I love and miss my daughter, being with her like this for any length of time is so emotionally and psychologically draining, I need my airbnb and time alone to come up for air briefly at the end of each day.

I go for a run while she heads back to her spot in the tunnels to get her things. When I come back, roughly three hours later, she's somehow filled the hotel room with *stuff*, several bike frames, a stack of bike tires, two industrial size garbage bags of what she tells me is laundry, and more. I'm in awe as to how she's managed this. It looks as though she's been living here for a month. My mind moves immediately to what check-out will be like; I know with absolute certainty that it's going to be chaos, and I dread being any part of it.

She spends several hours in the bathtub, and I listen to her singing and splashing from the other room. Periodically she calls out a question or giggles at a private joke. We order pizza and sit on the bed pretending everything is right with the world. But after I leave for the night, she calls me from the hotel room phone several times, convinced she has small pus-filled bumps all over her body and explains that she's trying to shave them off. This is obviously troubling, and I attempt to reassure her that she's okay, that I'm sure I would've noticed if there were anything to worry about, to please leave it until morning when I can help, that I'll see her soon, that I love her. She says "I love you, Mama" in a voice that tugs at me and brings tears when I hang up.

Sunday/Monday

When I get there in the morning Shyloh isn't there, but she's left me a note that she'll be back soon, so I wait, and soon she appears with even more bags of stuff. The day devolves from there, and she and I won't leave that hotel room together again for the rest of my visit.

By afternoon my own sanity feels threatened. She has voices intruding constantly, the majority of the time she is interacting with them and not me. And when she does talk to me, she roller-coasters from thankful that I'm there, to agitated or angry, to hostile. Now when I call her Shyloh, she snarls at me, "It's Grace!!" Her thoughts range from semi-reasonable to outrageous, and I fall repeatedly into trying to follow along with the trains of thought that seem sensible one moment only to be completely derailed the next. Several hours of this and finally I'm no longer able to engage with her and have to escape for a while. I don't know why, but the piles of laundry spread out on the floor really stress me out. She struggled almost a mile to bring these overstuffed bags full of clothes to her room and has declared several times that she needs to wash them but makes no effort to do so. There is a laundromat at the hotel, and time is ticking by. I tell her I would like to get the clothes washed for her and after a brief and rather dispassionate argument from her, she lets me. At last, I'm doing something that seems to make sense.

The hotel laundromat is a shabby little room with one washer and one dryer. I don't have any quarters and the change machine is out of order. The attendant at the desk in the lobby won't give me change. I run across the street to the 7-11. They won't give me change. The three businesses I try down the block won't give me change, all claiming a shortage due to

COVID and people switching to contactless payment systems. I'm irritated but haven't conceded defeat. Back in the laundry room I notice barcodes on both machines and realize I need to load an app and a credit card to use them. I consider how someone with no phone and no credit card is supposed to manage this. I download the app and proceed. Most of the clothes, as before, clearly aren't hers and some of the items are little more than rags and I throw these in the garbage can. When I finally finish several hours later, I've regained some emotional energy and am ready to go back to the room.

She pleads with me to *please* extend her hotel stay one more day. I try to explain that she'll then have to check out on her own since I will have already left, that if she loses her key they won't let her back into the room. But I don't have the energy to argue and finally agree. I decide I'm going to let this play out as it will, that this situation is far beyond my control anyway. And if I'm honest, I'm relieved that I'll miss the inevitable chaos when it's time for her to relinquish the room.

I've loaded more money onto Shyloh's card and she perks up at the prospect of using it to order groceries online. I bring my laptop to her room and she excitedly starts choosing things to add to her cart: deli chicken, salmon, bear-claw pastries, fruit smoothies, ice cream, granola, fruit loops, chips, cookies, sour gummies, chocolate milk. I remind her that she only has the small hotel refrigerator for a couple more days, that much of this is perishable, that the total is well over $200. I whittle the order down to just under $100, but reality seems to have dampened her enthusiasm. I go alone to pick up the order. When I return, she hardly looks up and doesn't eat any of it.

Shyloh sits on the bed doodling in her notebook or staring blankly, dozing off and on. She's muttering unintelligibly most of the time. She knows I'm there, but hasn't engaged with me in any meaningful way for several hours. I tell her I love her, that I'll see her in the morning, and leave around dark to return to my airbnb. She barely acknowledges me as I leave.

Back at my airbnb that night I finally break down. I call James and sob over the phone. The grief feels bottomless. What happened to approaching this with *acceptance and curiosity*? Clearly easier said than practiced. I'm determined to hold tightly to the tender moments Shyloh and I shared yesterday and the day before, as today threatens to push them aside.

The next day is much the same. Shyloh barely acknowledges me when I come in. She's sitting on the bed with her notebook and colored pencils and various open food containers spread around her.

"NO!" "What?" "I am not!" "What??" "No!" "NO!!" "What?"

I sit with a book and try to just be there, to observe, to respond when she does talk to me, but it's torture. My heart keeps flopping nonsensically in my chest. I leave in the late afternoon for a run. I tell her I love her and will see her in the morning.

Tuesday

She's not in the hotel room when I arrive the next morning. Somehow, there's even MORE trash here than yesterday. Again I marvel at her industriousness, even as I struggle to make sense of why she's brought it all here. The absurd clutter is too much for me to handle though, so I wait for her in the hotel parking lot with the bear-claws I'd bought us for breakfast. After about an hour I decide to leave the pastries on the bed with a note and walk down to the tunnels to see if she's there. She is. I can make out her silhouette at the end of the tunnel. I call out to her.

"Good morning," I start to say Shyloh, then quickly correct myself, "Grace!"

She snarls at me, "What the fuck?? No! Go the fuck away! Go!!"

I feel like I've been punched in the face. I'm absolutely not prepared to handle conflict again so soon this morning. I turn around without a word and go for a long walk.

After a couple hours I'm ready to try again and head back to the hotel, hoping she's there and has calmed down too. She's there but has bolted the door and won't let me in. Again she snarls at me to go home, to go back to Wisconsin, to leave her alone, ". . . just fucking go away!" I argue through the door that I don't understand, to please let me in. I remind her that she'll need to check out tomorrow at noon, that I am leaving early tomorrow morning and won't be here to help, that they won't let her back in the room if she loses her key. Relenting, I slide my key under the door, reminding myself that

I'd decided to let this play out, that it is beyond my control. Still, it feels like I'm giving up, like I'm abandoning her. I spend the morning walking around San Diego, then drive out to the nature reserve and try to run. I feel numb and my heart won't stop its erratic pounding. I call James and cry some more. Back at my airbnb I pack and clean the apartment, then watch brainless TV until I finally fall asleep.

She calls me at 1 a.m. from her hotel room phone. "I miss you, Mama. Have a safe trip. Please come back?"

"I love you," I say.

"Good night, I love you too, Mama."

Of course I will come back. I won't ever stop trying to find her.

Wednesday

I'm sitting at the airport in Denver during a long layover thinking about Shyloh, and also the mess in the hotel room. I consider that maybe the police will be called, that maybe she'll be combative or psychotic enough for them to take her in on a 5150. It occurs to me suddenly that she may have been, consciously or not, protecting us both from a repeat of my last visit by wanting to stay in the room until after I'd left. The thought makes me cry. I also can't help the feeling that my showing up in her world might make things harder for her. There are moments she is clearly overjoyed to have me

near, but I can see the anguish it causes her too, to be reminded of what she's left behind, to perceive her world through
my eyes, to say goodbye.

I can't stop worrying that she won't be there at check-
out and will get locked out with her things inside. Most of
the garbage in the room I know will be abandoned, but she
does have a small backpack of essentials, her journal, sketch
book, and I'm thinking especially of her wallet with the
debit card I'd just given her. It's not quite noon and I finally
decide I need to at least call the hotel to explain the situation, that I'd rented the room for my daughter, that I've left
the state but she is still there. I explain that she is mentally
ill and that there will likely be an issue at checkout. I ask
if their policy is to call the police. When they say yes, I assure them she isn't dangerous and would they please request
PERT instead, hoping she will be evaluated and potentially
receive treatment. I give them my number and ask them to
please call if anything happens.

As luck would have it my flight is delayed and so my
phone is on when the hotel calls three hours later to confirm
that I've given permission to allow her back in to get her
things. As I'd suspected she showed up an hour past check-
out, caused a scene, and the police were called. I don't know
if PERT was called too, if she was evaluated for psychiatric
care, but she is ultimately let back in to retrieve what she
deems important. Most of what filled the room, though, is left
behind for the maids to deal with.

Sketched by Grace (Shyloh)

MONEY TO BURN – JANUARY 2021

It's been nearly two months. I'm pleasantly surprised that she still has her card and has even managed to buy and set up a phone. She leaves it off most of the time, but I love that she can send me pictures and poems again, and that we can talk as long as we want when she does call, if the battery's been sufficiently charged. This also means she can call and text with frequent requests (often ranting demands) that I put more money on her card.

My initial plan is to set Shyloh's FamZoo account to automatically load her card with a weekly allowance and I start with $100 per week, imagining this will incentivize her to "adult" and spend wisely, but it soon becomes clear that $100 isn't going to be enough. I increase it to $250 per week, but the money is often gone in a day or two, and she inevitably calls for more. When Shyloh uses her debit card, I get a text alert with the amount, place of purchase and the balance, and I often see that she's spent it all at Dollar Store or Walmart and I flash back to the spending spree I'd witnessed during my last visit, and cringe. But when she calls a day or two later and asks for $20 more so she can get some food, and then the next day another $30 for some other necessity, I comply. So instead of weekly I decide to make it a daily allowance, determined to pick an amount and stick to it.

She goes for weeks sometimes without communicating with me at all, and those daily text alerts from her card are little messages that tell me she's okay, that she's eating, that she's alive. I cherish those little messages.

When she does eventually lose the card, I order her a new one and, again, the trick is getting it to her with no ID or address to send it to, back to problem solving mode.

I reach out to James' cousin who's recently moved to San Diego, and she's willing to help. While we wait for the new card to arrive, I figure out ways to order groceries and load Shyloh's 7-11 account from my computer with the card information. It's a daily challenge and I'm relieved when the new card finally arrives. I mail it to James's cousin. We arrange for a convenient place and time for them to meet, easier now that Shyloh has a phone. Amazingly, it all goes perfectly without a hitch.

Shyloh has always had a smooth clear complexion, but she's been complaining of disturbingly oily skin lately, especially on her face. She describes how squeezing the skin on her cheek or forehead results in a profuse oozing of oil from her pores. It's unclear if this is a hallucination, as I'd suspected the "pus-filled bumps" from a couple months ago were, but I do some Google searching and learn that excessive sun exposure, which she surely experiences, can cause overactive *sebaceous glands* (small oil producing glands attached to hair follicles just under the skin) with symptoms similar to what she's describing. I relay this information and suggest perhaps she start using a high SPF sunscreen. She responds with a poem:

> **I was thinking a fancy floppy hat**
> **Perhaps, or parasol.**
> **Interesting factoids,**
> **What's a 'sebaceous' mean though?**

She still makes me smile.

I have been reading a lot about *schizoaffective disorder/ bipolar type*, Shyloh's most recent diagnosis. People with this disorder experience psychotic symptoms, such as hallucinations or delusions, as well as episodes of mania and sometimes depression. Some sources note that it's unclear if this is simply the overlaying of a psychotic disorder with a mood disorder, or if it's truly its own illness, but the defining features include *a major mood episode of depression and/or mania, and a minimum of two weeks of psychotic symptoms without the mood episodes*. Because the timing of symptoms is part of the diagnosis, it's recommended that symptoms be tracked, and since I've been able to talk with her fairly regularly lately, I've been able to recognize patterns to her moods and behaviors and how these correlate to when she goes MIA for several weeks at a time. Shyloh used to track her mood swings too, before she went to California and also during the nine months she was in jail, but I'm not sure she's able to distinguish these changes anymore. She says instead that she's "tuned into the frequencies." She comments that being able to talk with me regularly has made her feel more in touch with reality, but there is a rushed, urgent quality to her speech.

Friday she calls asking for $400 to rent a room for the weekend. She's insistent, and I finally agree. She assures me she's doing GREAT!

By Sunday she's spent it all, on what exactly isn't clear but not sure it included the room, and she calls pleading that she needs $150 more, again to rent a room. Her speech is forced and erratic, slurred, and her reasoning is hard to follow, but she's adamant that she needs the room.

By Tuesday morning she is "tuned into the frequencies" and ranting something about being kicked out of her hotel room, accused of breaking into someone else's room and the police had been called. She sounds frantic and delusional.

Haven't heard from her for three days, wonder if she's been taken in on a psychiatric hold?

Friday afternoon she texts that she needs money for an Uber, that she is on a road trip with a couple friends for the weekend, and sends me a selfie with two strangers in the background, a couple she's just met.

This continues to snowball and I start to panic when five days and roughly $1500 later, most of it spent on Ubers, she calls from Santa Barbara, about 100 miles north of Los Angeles along the coast, needing "just a little more so I can get back to SD."

It's hard to explain what happens, how I get pulled in with her. I don't understand it myself. It should be easy to say no and hang up, but it isn't always. I think some of the difficulty relates to my inability to figure out definitively where the line is, or if there even is – or should be – one. She gets into predicaments that do require more money to resolve, and then she ends up in another predicament that requires even more. It doesn't just snowball – to me, it feels like an avalanche. I get impossibly tangled in the system's insistence that it's her life, her choices, that she's an adult, and I have no right to impose my wishes on her; this is what the law says after all. She isn't always asking for money; sometimes she even goes for a week at a time with a positive balance on her card. And it isn't that I never say "no" to her demands. I do quite often actually. But sometimes I don't have the energy to push back. And, well, it's her money.

I'm relieved when she makes it back to San Diego a few days later, back on her own familiar ground. But this recent adventure has given her the grand idea that she and I should Uber back to Wisconsin together, something about wanting me in the backseat with her, that if I'm driving I'll "always be the Mom." I can't decipher what she means, but after initially disregarding the Uber idea as ridiculous, I begin to consider it. How feasible would it be?

(poem received by text early one morning)
... sorrowful your day may be
Yet choice for otherwise is as simple as it is moving
Choose which ever keeps you steadily moving forth
-Grace

ACCEPTANCE – MARCH 2021

Each trip to see her seems to teach me a new lesson in acceptance. I am witnessing a slow and steady downward spiral, and it's unnerving how the previously unthinkable begins to lean towards normal. I suspect this happens for her too.

It's so hard to explain what it's like to be with her, the conflicting emotions and terrible toll it takes on my psyche. How in the same moment I can be overcome with love and relief to have her close, with anxiety and worry for her situation, with anger and guilt as I struggle to find acceptance in what she and I are both experiencing. At the same time, I fight the selfish desire to flee. My own mind starts to question what's real; she draws me in and leaves me abandoned in her chaos. I am reminded of the specialized brain cells called *mirror neurons*, thought to be part of the physiology behind empathy, and I consider how in the moment my fragmenting mind is trying to mirror hers.

PACIFIC BEACH – MARCH 2021

Now that she has a phone, it's much easier to orchestrate this visit. She's waiting for me at the 7-11 near the Pacific Beach boardwalk, rocking back and forth on her skateboard, and smoking a cigarette. After a quick hug she hands me a keychain trinket, a tiny jeweled flip-flop with San Diego engraved into the sole and a miniature jigsaw puzzle attached in a small plastic tube.

"An early birthday present," she says with a half smile. She and I used to do jigsaws frequently when she was a kid, the big ones, 1500 or 2000 pieces. She was always really good at puzzles. When they were done, I'd help her carefully transfer and glue them to cardboard to hang on her bedroom walls. I bought her a large portable puzzle case so she could work on them anywhere, and every year for her birthday and Christmas I'd search for a new puzzle, something grand with fiery dragons or breathtaking mountain scenes, or butterflies. I brought a puzzle with me on one of my recent trips to visit her, thinking it might be something we could do together, but she no longer shows any interest in them.

Shyloh suggests we walk the half mile to the Salvation Army so she can get some new clothes and for the next couple hours the two of us peruse the racks like old times. On the way back to my car, she declares we should just Uber to the airbnb instead, reluctant to get in the car with me driving. Abruptly, she says she needs to get something and points to the jogging stroller parked next to a bus stop across the street, her recent flea market purchase. It's got a tattered green top and one of the wheels is flat, and I notice she's attached a padlock to the wheel but hasn't actually locked it to anything. In the past she's declared defiantly that she never panhandles and doesn't push a cart, and seems embarrassed to have me with her while she pushes this, so instead she tells me she'll meet me at my airbnb later. I suggest I can pick her up, but when I ask where she's staying she snaps, "None of your business!" She then softens and suggests instead that we meet up in the morning.

My heart has been "lub-Dubbing" cooperatively since I had the ablation done, and I head to the nature reserve for a satisfying run to decompress before settling into my airbnb for the night.

Shyloh keeps her phone turned off most of the time and I'm unclear on when and where we're meeting the next day. She texts early to tell me she's making sandcastles, and I assume I'm to infer she'll be on the beach somewhere, but there's a lot of sand in Pacific Beach. I wander for over an hour before I see her jogging stroller parked along a curb. I eventually run into her in an alley nearby collecting cans. She is angry with me for not having found her sooner. Baffled and a little angry now myself, I follow behind as she belligerently ignores me and continues her collecting. Eventually she stops at a liquor store. When she comes out we walk together to a grassy spot near where she parked her stroller and we sit in the shade together. She's bought Ramen-in-a-Cup and a mini bottle of liquor, and after ingesting both her mood improves.

During one of her "adulting" moments several weeks ago, Shyloh acknowledged that having an ID would greatly simplify her life, allowing her to get her own hotel rooms, pick up mail, potentially travel back to Wisconsin by train or airplane, and she agreed then that this would be one of our adulting goals this visit. I researched the steps involved and what documents we would need, hoping to simplify the process as much as possible, but there will be a lot of hoops to jump through. I ordered her a new birth certificate and SS card and scrambled to figure out how to produce two proofs of residency when she has no address. I made an appointment for this morning at a homeless service that offers these verifications, and pre-registered for an appointment at the DMV this afternoon. I've reminded Shyloh repeatedly about these appointments and reminded her again yesterday to be sure she had time to wrap her brain around the idea when the time came, and she seemed prepared yesterday. Sitting here now I remind her again that if we're going to keep our appointments we'll have to leave soon, but it's obvious the whole prospect is beginning to overwhelm her. She starts making excuses and arguing, and we let the appointed time slip past. I give her the documents to hold on to, pretending that she won't lose them, that she'll go to the DMV on her own.

She is visibly relieved with the looming ID task behind us, and we walk together as she shows me around her new neighborhood. I still see the person I know and love, that beautiful, engaging and big-hearted soul, glimpses intertwined with this new person who calls herself Grace. Grace is paranoid, often angry, disorganized in her thinking. Sometimes she tells me she doesn't know me, "Who the fuck are you anyway?! What the fuck do you want from me?!" And then she'll walk away, no comment, no explanation, as though she forgets I'm there.

But today, for the most part, Shyloh is here. At one point, joyously pointing out the flowers she loves, she asks me my favorites, and later that night while I am sleeping and she is out wandering, she picks a few and makes me a small bouquet that she hangs in a tree along the route she knows we'll take the next day. She generously offers to share whatever she has, not just with me, but with anyone. "I got this for you," she says, and hands me a trinket, or a candy bar, a bottle of water, a seashell.

We stop into a small shop that sells knick-knacks, glass pipes, hip clothes, and jewelry. Shyloh shows me her wire-wrapped pendants for sale on consignment, hanging on the rack above the counter. She proudly introduces me to the owner, and my heart brims with a pride of its own for this talented, clever, and beautiful woman who is my daughter.

Shyloh remains convinced we should hire an Uber for the drive back to Wisconsin, and I'm still not sure how feasible it is to find drivers to take us that far, but nonetheless she wants us to practice traveling together. Another of her goals during this visit is for us to take an Uber day trip somewhere. With this in mind, for my last day in California I've reserved a small loft apartment for the two of us in a rural community about an hour west of San Diego. It's at a farm for rescued animals with horses, ponies, goats, chickens and rabbits. Shyloh had lots of pets when she was a kid and took riding lessons briefly when she was twelve, winning a blue ribbon at the first and only riding competition she entered. I know that close contact with animals can have a powerful impact on troubled hearts and minds, and I hope that this short adventure out of the city together might also be a healing experience for her.

Our trip to the farm is tomorrow, but when I remind her she wavers and wonders instead if we could get a hotel room nearby. We're walking along the boardwalk and pass an upscale hotel, its courtyard pool and hot tub facing the ocean. Shyloh comments how often she's passed this hotel, always wondering what it would be like to watch the people walking by while soaking in that hot tub. She brightens, then pleads "can't we please, please, please? Something fancy?" It's her money but my frugal brain is balking, and the responsible adult me opposes the idea. But a conflicting part of me wants to pamper her. Just this once, that would be okay wouldn't it? So we go inside to inquire.

As we step into the shiny lobby, I am struck with a sudden shame and embarrassment for Shyloh's sake, for her grimy fingernails and unwashed hair and subtle body odor, and a hot anger rises up directed at the polite woman working the hotel desk, with her perfect manicure, stylish coiffure and perfumed air, and at myself. I register for two nights.

Our fourth floor balcony faces the parking lot instead of the ocean as we'd hoped, but Shyloh's mood has buoyed and she wants to dress up, suggests we go out to dinner tonight, her treat. She takes a three hour bath and asks me tentatively if I'd wash her back for her. These days she doesn't want to be touched, and I feel privileged by the request. She is clearly ashamed of her nakedness and her filth and keeps apologizing and seems so small and vulnerable sitting hunched in that tub. I savor the tender moment of being close to her, of offering such intimate care as I gently suds her back.

I go for a run while she soaks and when I come back, she's dressed and asks me to braid her hair. Both sides of her head are shaved but the mohawk down the center sports hair about five inches long and I do my best to French braid this. She's also been shaving off one of her eyebrows lately, convinced there's an infection in her brow, and hands me an eye liner pencil, asking if I would draw on her missing eyebrow to match the other. She's put a lot of effort into her appearance for our evening out. She looks nice, and it feels like a gesture of love and trust and a longing for better times.

We walk around Pacific Beach as darkness falls, like two vacationing tourists looking for a place to eat. Neither of us is very hungry, but I sense we both yearn to hold onto the relative normalcy we're experiencing. We find a little seafood spot and chat comfortably during dinner, and everything just feels so ... normal. We decide this will be our new tradition; each time I visit we will come to this restaurant and do this again. When the check comes, she proudly pulls out her debit card and pays.

I cherish these pleasant moments with her, but they also make the troubling ones harder to understand and accept. After dinner, her composure unravels and she abruptly leaves me standing on the street corner. I head back to my airbnb, comforted in knowing that at least Shyloh will have a comfortable place to spend the night. She texts me later, "Good night, Mama. I love you!"

She's in the bathtub again when I get to her hotel room the next morning. It's soon clear she won't be accompanying me to the farm today, so I lie back on one of the beds and consider staying here with her tonight instead. She's in a bad mood and her voices annoyingly interrupt our intermittent conversations. At one point she looks at me and says, accusingly, "What do you want to know?? Ask me!" I'm taken aback.

There is so, so much I ache to know, and yet because I don't know what to ask first, I ask nothing.

At some point in the afternoon I bring up mental illness and *schizoaffective disorder*, suggesting that medications would likely help her to focus again, would help to dampen the voices so they're not constantly interfering. She's incredulous at first, says she knows people with schizophrenia, that no, her problem is the drugs. I agree, the meth she uses has most surely caused damage, but I'm convinced she's been self-medicating all along, and that her mind went over the edge along with the bus. She's quiet for a while; my words seem to have sunk in. Then she gets up and says she needs to have a "selfish moment" and goes out the door. I assume she's going for a cigarette, but when she comes back she keeps nodding out, clearly high. I suspect heroin, or its more potent cousin fentanyl, and then she's sleeping. I'm no longer considering staying with her in the hotel room. I know she uses, but I refuse to be present like this while she does; I drew that particular line long ago, and she has crossed it.

So after several hours watching her sleep, and confident she hasn't overdosed, I decide to go to the farm alone and leave her a note.

She texts me late afternoon, says she'll catch an Uber and meet me at the farm, then an hour later changes her mind again. I suggest I come pick her up but she's reluctant to get in the car with me driving in "the Mom seat," and we go back and forth like this all evening. I suggest that I could drive there, leave the car, and we could Uber back together, but it's nearly 10 p.m. now and none of it even makes sense anymore. I reassure her I'll be there first thing in the morning and we say goodnight.

She texts again much later, long rambling texts, pleading with me to stay with her in San Diego. "... Pleasepleaseplease, I need you, Mama. I NEED YOU! Don't leave!"

Fuck, how can a broken heart keep breaking?

When I get to her room the next morning, she's in the bathroom and there are a couple other people just leaving, explaining that Grace had invited them to sleep there and to use the shower. They are shaggy and disheveled but now their bodies at least are clean. They are both polite and speak very highly of Shyloh, of Grace, and when I introduce myself as her mom, "You two look alike." The room is a mess, and I'm again awed at how quickly it happens. There are boxes of discarded day-old bakery goods, dirty clothes, beer and soda bottles, wrappers and cigarette butts, and the garbage cans are overflowing. One mattress has been pulled onto the floor as an extra bed, and another bed has been made out on the balcony with one of the comforters. I'm compelled to straighten up but Shyloh retorts uncharacteristically, "Leave it! That's what maids are for. It's their job!" I do my best to pick up anyway. The nice outfit she'd worn a couple nights ago lies in a pile in the closet and I remind her not to forget the clothes, but she says she doesn't want them, that they're dirty. Her jogging stroller made it into the room

at some point during the night and I suggest she throw the
clothes in there, she could wash them later, reminding her
that the outfit had looked so nice on her, but she argues that
then all her stuff will smell like dirty clothes. There are full
water bottles bought from room service scattered around the
room and she doesn't seem concerned with taking these either, and I can't make any sense of what she's choosing to
keep and what she's leaving behind. I remind myself again
that much of this is beyond my control. I force myself to
step back and let the maids deal with what's left behind. She
never did soak in the hotel's courtyard hot tub.

I assume we're headed for a coffee as I help her get the
stroller into the elevator and out the lobby door. She dips
into the alley behind the hotel to grab an old rusty bike that I
presume she'd left the night before, and spends the next several minutes trying to attach the neglected bike to the jogging stroller. The stroller has only one hitch, the other having been broken off at some point, and there's no mounted
hardware, so she uses a piece of wire to connect the stroller's frame to one side of the rear wheel's axle and begins
walking the bike down the side of the road. The stroller is
more dragged than towed, but amazingly it works, as long
as she doesn't turn left. She's ignoring me and walking determinedly ahead, so I follow quietly. When we arrive at a
small bike shop, Shyloh steps inside briefly and when she
comes out the owner meets us in the alley along the side of
the building and hands her a hand pump to fill the bike's
flat tires. They discuss derailers and new rims, as though

the bike they're looking at isn't held together with rust, and he comments thoughtfully that the bike's tubes won't likely hold the air for long.

"Any time, Grace," he says when she hands him back the pump, and we move again down the sidewalk. I note that she seems less self-conscious pulling her cart than pushing it. It is comforting to know there are so many people here that are kind to her. I'm sure that not everyone is.

There's a little café down the block. We stop in for coffee and I buy us both something to eat. It feels like there's so much we need to say to each other, but we'd need so much more time together to get there and I need to leave for the airport in half an hour. All I can do is promise that I'll be back. I can feel by her subtle stiffness as we hug that she's uncomfortable with the contact, but I squeeze her to my chest anyway. We part then, me to my car and then the airport, she to somewhere unknown to me, pushing a rusty bike with flat tires, her stroller dragging behind.

On the flight home, I decide to increase her daily allowance to $100. I don't know anymore if there's any point to trying so hard to save the money. I can't get her to acknowledge that we should think of tomorrow. I try to explain to her that thinking of tomorrow is my job, that I'm doing my best. Sometimes she thanks me for being the adult, commends me, and says I'm doing an awesome job. Most of the time, though, she rails and rants that it's her money and who the fuck do I think I am. She asserts that she's absolutely fine with the fact that when it's gone it's gone, that she'll just go back to living out of dumpsters, and until then she doesn't want to be hungry, doesn't want to want for anything. I feel intensely the need to do whatever I can to ease her existence. I feel so powerless to help in any meaningful way most of the time.

We text off and on over the next several weeks. I send her a picture of the completed miniature puzzle she gave me; she sends me a sketch, a self-portrait with the caption "If found, just call my Mom." I send her a photo of the crocuses that have started pushing up through the remaining snow; she sends me a picture of a peach colored rose bush in full bloom. She texts to tell me her stroller has been stolen, ". . . just an FYI if you feel any stress waves from my way. That's why. Man, I'm Irritated! Oh well, I'm rebuilding (literally) and at this moment am using the last daylight to work on a project. Love you." I ask what the project is and she replies the next day, "Knife pocket mirror," whatever that means.

Nothing for a week, then, "Heya. Just turned the device back on. So you won't worry I'm checking in. I love you, Mama."

She calls on her birthday ten days later and I tell her I've got a week free at the end of the month, that I've made plans to fly out again to see her, that we'll celebrate her birthday belatedly. She tells me she's more or less in the same area, and we hang up with "Love you, see you soon!"

In the meantime, my nonprofit is again hosting the state

tournament this summer, and we had opened boxer registration a few weeks ago. Last year's tournament was canceled due to COVID, just as we were heading to the venue to set up the ring, and we're struggling to regain that momentum. I appreciate the distraction. Without it I drive myself crazy, though thankfully my heart is "lub-Dubbing" along obediently, no longer creating a racing anxiety of its own.

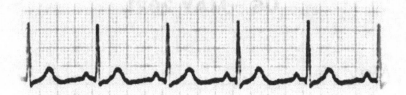

REMEMBERING FOR THE BOTH OF US – MAY 2021

May 26

I fly out to San Diego again tomorrow. I'm hoping she'll call again so I can confirm she remembers I'm coming and decide on a meeting spot, but I haven't heard anything from her since her birthday. I'm worried she's lost her phone. She's been using her debit card though, so my plan is to use the text alerts to get a bead on her general location and to search from there. I have a good grasp on the neighborhood and am feeling pretty confident I will find her.

May 27

My flight is uneventful. I get off the plane and head to pick up the rental car, but when I show my driver's license at the counter, it's handed back to me with a negative shake of the head. I realize I mistakenly grabbed the expired one from my wallet when I left this morning. I'm suddenly aware that I'm 2000 miles from home without a valid ID and I can't help note the irony of this. How had I managed to get on the plane this morning? I recall the guy at security had done a double take when checking my license but hadn't commented. Fuck. Adrenaline starts dumping. I call James at work and ask if he could check my wallet at home, to send me a photo of my valid license so I can at least rent the car. A quick Google search while I'm waiting and I see that yes, you can board a plane with an expired driver's license with a one-year grace period.

Grace. I see that word everywhere these days.

Thirty minutes later James texts me the photo of my valid license, I rent the car, I'm back on track. The brief adrenaline dump has left me feeling a little drained, and I rally my confidence as I head to the airbnb to drop off my stuff and then to Pacific Beach to find her.

I envision her in the spots where she and I hung out together the last time I was here, imagining how good it will be to see her again so soon, to hug her, picturing her delighted surprise when she looks up and sees me. I start at the 7-11, half expecting to see her there on her skateboard waiting for me like last time. She's not, but there's a guy hanging around on a bike in the parking lot in front of the store and I ask if by any chance he knows Grace?

"No, sorry." I walk up towards the ocean boardwalk and as the ocean comes into view I'm struck with the magnitude of everything, not just of trying to find her but of trying to save her, of everything, and I feel a wave of panic threatening my confidence. I push the feeling away and focus.

Back at the 7-11 the guy on the bike approaches me, asks if I need help. I tell him that Grace is my daughter, that I have traveled from Wisconsin to visit, that she doesn't have a phone and I don't know where to find her. I show him a picture and he tells me I look like her. He tells me that he and his buddies usually ride up and down the boardwalk all night, that he'll keep his eyes open. If he sees her he'll give her the message to call me. We exchange phone numbers.

Encouraged, I throw my small backpack over my shoulder and continue walking, watching for people who look like they might know her, for other folks that live out here like she does. I consider this: What is it exactly that makes them stand out?

Some of the unhoused are obvious, with shopping carts of precariously balanced treasures, bodies and clothes filthy, often passionately arguing with themselves. Others are much less obvious. Maybe their clothes are dirty, wrinkled, don't quite match, but no, that's not it. I've learned about all the perfectly sound, stylish clothes that can be found in dumpsters, and I know firsthand that Goodwill is overflowing with clean, practically new threads. Shyloh continuously amazes me with her creative sense of style and how relatively put together she can make herself look, even out here. So, what is it? Yes, their hair might be unkempt, fingernails dirty, they are almost always carrying at least a backpack, often toting a bike or skateboard. But also, they lack that rushed overscheduled quality that people with jobs and rent and bills to pay have; they are searching but not hurried. I think it is in their faces, in their eyes, a weariness, a defiance, trying to exist invisibly but yearning to be seen. I have been asked a couple times already since I've been here if I'm homeless, if I need help. Maybe my eyes have this look too.

I walk the neighborhoods, the alleys, the parks, and ask if anyone knows Grace. It's getting easier to use the name, but it sticks in my throat a little, tugs at my heart, every time I say that I'm "Grace's mom." Most of the people I talk to are at first guarded and reserved, but after I explain who I am, I'm touched by how compassionate and concerned they are for me and my mission. Everyone I meet that knows her comments that I look like her; one guy says she and I talk alike, have the same laugh. But no one has seen her for several days. I see a couple people camped out off the main street, along a half wall that spans the short block. One guy looks familiar. I remember him from the last time I was out here. He sits and rants loudly to himself today, his possessions scattered haphazardly around him on the sidewalk. I don't bother asking him if he's seen my daughter; he's clearly absorbed by his own journey.

I check the businesses that she's used her card at in the past month. Most of the attendants say they recognize her but haven't seen her for several days. I ask them to please tell her to call her mom if they see her.

She hasn't used her card since I've been here and I'm running out of places to look. There are moments when I catch glimpses of the impossibility of what I'm doing, and feel the tears building. I'm holding back a tidal wave of emotion, but won't allow the luxury of letting it go just yet. It's getting dark and I'm exhausted, my feet are sore, and I'm hungry. I envision Shyloh sitting here on this same piece of grass, contemplating this same view, exhausted and hungry, her feet sore, her heart aching. I feel close to her, knowing that I'm seeing, breathing, existing in this place.

I decide to call it a day. My phone says I've put on eleven miles this afternoon.

I'm crawling into bed when I get an alert from a nearby deli that she's used the card there moments ago. I call the deli and ask if they could please try to catch her but when I call back a few minutes later I'm told they just missed her. I get another call as I'm falling asleep, from the guy on the bike at the 7-11. He's calling to let me know that they've been look-ing for my daughter for hours, haven't seen her but have run into quite a few folks who know her and have put the word out. He tells me they'll keep looking. I'm touched that he thought to call me to let me know this.

"I can't imagine how hard this must be, what you're go-ing through," he says. I don't dwell on his comment, but I couldn't have imagined it either.

May 28

I'm up at 4 a.m. still exhausted but can't sleep, so I make coffee and drive to the deli, the last place I knew her to be. I check the public restroom doors at a few spots, knowing that people often sleep there if they can get away with it – running water, a roof, a door to lock. They were all unoccupied this morning though.

I get an alert that she's made a purchase at a grocery store several blocks away, and I head in that direction on foot. As I pass the block with the half wall, I see the familiar man still sitting on the sidewalk engaged in his tirade, and then I see another person sitting along the wall farther down, a woman. I recognize her silhouette, something familiar about the way she's moving and I'm overcome with relief as I get closer and see that it's her. I've found her.

She looks up as I near, but there's no delighted look of surprise on her face, no bittersweet and tearful hug.

"Fuck no. No! NO! You fucking kidding me?? No. Go! Get out of here!! I didn't invite you. NO!"

Stunned, I shakily try to sit down next to her.

"Don't fucking sit down here. Rude! Go away! Leave!" She starts packing up her things. "Fine," she grumbles, "I was leaving anyway."

I'm in absolute shock, gut punched, at a total loss for how to respond and I start pleading with her. Please, let's just talk for a bit, please wait, I don't understand, please wait! Please don't leave!

She snarls, "I'm busy, I've got shit to do! I don't know you! We're not even FRIENDS!"

"What? I'm your mom, I love you, I don't understand! Wait, please don't leave!"

"Okay fine, I love you too, now just go home, ANDREA!"

I'm so completely untethered, baffled, in absolute disbelief of what is happening. She's gathered her several bags of belongings and has them hanging from both arms as she rides away into traffic on her bike, one hand on the handlebar, the other holding up the iced coffee she's just purchased.

I start jogging along beside the bike, not knowing what else to do, pleading with her to stop, to explain. Weaving through traffic, she leaves me standing there on the corner with my heart stuck in my throat.

The familiar guy sitting along the wall nearby is silent now, looking at me with pained empathy in his eyes and he quietly asks me if I'm okay. All I can do is stand there and sob.

I walk along the ocean for a while, feeling empty and lost and confused. I don't know how to frame what I've just experienced. I don't even have words for what this feels like. I think about all the men and women that I've met these past couple years in my effort to keep Shyloh in my life, young and old, living out here on the streets like my daughter, most of them addicts, many of them mentally ill. And I think about their mothers.

I approach a small group of people in the small bay park where Shyloh and I spent afternoons the last time I visited. Noticing several small clusters of bedding, clothes and other belongings under the eaves of a public shower house, I assume at least a few of these people are living here. Several of the guys are working on bikes. I've learned that most of the folks in this area travel either by bike or skateboard, and readily sell and trade in stolen bikes and parts. This neighborhood, in fact, is known for its alarmingly high rate of bike theft.

Initially the group is guarded, but a couple people recognize me from my likeness to Shyloh. I share some of my story, that I've come from Wisconsin to find and spend time with my daughter, Sh – Grace. I'm invited to sit and when I ask, they share their stories too.

John, a 60-year-old former high school history teacher from San Francisco, tells me he'd come to San Diego with his parents as a teen and loved it. He says he's only known Grace a couple months but has a deep respect for her. Says she's a loner, often unapproachable, that she's tough as hell and has earned her place in the street hierarchy. He's taken it upon himself to help me find her and pushes his bike alongside me as we walk, taking periodic swigs from the small bottle in his jacket. He tells me he worked his way back down to San Diego after his marriage failed and he'd lost his job several years ago. He has a daughter about Shyloh's age but confesses that she hates him. I suspect alcohol has played a leading role in why he's here. This former teacher still has his intellect and is very articulate, but John is a bike thief now. He tells me he's hooked my daughter up with bikes now and then and confesses that he's stolen them from her too.

"We take care of each other out here, but yea, we steal from each other all the time too." John tells me he tries to help my daughter out when he can, that she seems very sad, that she cries a lot but won't let anyone comfort her, "and what a soulful voice she has." Sometimes she'll let him sit nearby as she sings quietly to herself.

Georgia seems a bit like the matriarch of this little group. Age is hard to guess out here – the elements aren't kind to people's faces – but I figure she's about my age. She has a friendly brindle pit-mix who loyally shares her life and eagerly accepts belly rubs from anyone who offers. I ask Georgia what brought her here. She tells me she came to town from Los Angeles several months ago, that her car was towed and her phone died, and she's been living here ever since. Her rationalizations for why she's still here don't make much sense and the more I talk with her the clearer it becomes that she too is struggling with addiction and most likely mental illness. She also confesses that she has a son, and I can see her eyes well up when she tells me she hasn't heard from him in years. When she was in jail, she explains, she'd broken ties with him, told him not to call or write, not wanting to subject him to her misery, and now she doesn't know where to find him anymore. I try to overlay her story on mine.

I woke this morning with an insight, as though Shyloh had come to me in my dreams. A realization that the life Shyloh has built here requires a full commitment to her illnesses that would make remembering and holding on to anything she's left behind nearly impossible to integrate. I believe she pushed me away so insistently yesterday to resist any seepage of my reality through the cracks of hers. I am confident I know her heart, and believe she is desperately protecting it.

And so I decide to take on the burden and sorrow of remembering for the both of us. I am her mama bear after all.

It's midmorning and I head back down to Pacific Beach, no real plan in mind. It's Memorial Day weekend and there are people everywhere, vacationing families, amorous couples, strutting and barely clothed singles. With vague curiosity I consider their lives.

I get another text alert from the same grocery store and head in that direction, hoping to see her again, hopeful that yesterday was an anomaly, hopeful but apprehensive. And again, by some fated stroke I see her, reclined across a boulder along the boardwalk near the ocean, eating cut fruit. My heart pounds as I approach, more slowly this time, respectful not to intrude on her breakfast, hoping she'll let me sit with her for a bit. She looks up and sees me, and without a word or another glance she packs up her things. I protest – No no, it's okay. I'll go, you don't have to leave – but she's already gone.

I sit down in the void she's left and let the tears flow.

I spend the rest of the day in my room. I don't have the motivation to go for a run like I'd planned, or to go walking, or to eat, or shower, or talk to anyone, to do anything but sit here. I find myself sobbing off and on. I feel either utter bewildering sadness or nothing at all. Periodically during the day I remind myself that this heartache that's engulfed me is a part of what I said I'd hold onto, would cherish, that this is the burden and sorrow of remembering. And so I hold the last sight of her in my mind, reclining across that boulder, wiry and tan and still beautiful, like a hungry lioness. I cling to how it felt to find her there, and how it felt when she got up and left.

Shyloh, 32 years old, Pacific Beach

THE PHONE CALL – JUNE 11, 2021

She calls me from Goodwill, having asked to use their phone. It's the first time we've spoken since that morning a month ago when she rode away and left me standing bewildered on the street corner, and my heart immediately swells with relief to hear her voice, even as I brace for whatever might come next. She asks apologetically for a little extra money on her debit card so she can buy another bike. The last one's been stolen, she says. She asks what I am doing, and I know that we will chat now for as long as the store clerk allows.

I tell her I am painting the downstairs bathroom, the one next to the small guest room that I redecorated for her a couple years ago. I remind her of the small writing desk I placed under the window looking out at a flower garden, the favorite framed painting of a sunflower on the wall next to the bed, ready for her when she finally comes home. I ask her what color I should paint the bathroom walls and she describes to me the brilliance of the perfect blue sky, visible through the store's window, how vivid the palm tree green is as it touches the blue. We decide together it would be fun to paint a sky blue wall with just the tops of the trees coming up from the floor, as though looking down on them from the clouds. I hear the store clerk in the background impatiently asking her to return the phone. Before we hang up, I tell her cautiously how glad I am to hear from her, how much I love her. "I love you too, Mama." There's a pause and she says again, "I love you."

I don't see her morning coffee purchase when I check her debit card the next day, none of her regular daily snacks. Nothing the following day, or the day after that. I have an annoying tickle of worry that something is wrong. Damn, I bet she's lost her card again.

It's Sunday afternoon, three days since her call from Goodwill, when my phone rings, a California area code on the caller ID. I answer expectantly, assuming it's Shyloh calling from a borrowed phone.

"Ms. Nelson? I'm so sorry to have to tell you this ..."

No, wait ... I'm struggling to unhear.

JUNE 13, 2021

Her body was found by a woman who lived in a neighboring tent. The Medical Examiner Investigator explains delicately but frankly that she had likely been dead for several days, that she'd been unrecognizable, labeled a Jane Doe initially until prints later identified her. Cause of death is also unclear, though I think we all assume it to have been an overdose. Fentanyl deaths have been epidemic in California lately. I'm told toxicology will take several months to come back. I ask about Shyloh's things, if anything was retrieved from the tent, knowing she always had a small backpack with her everywhere she went, always carried a sketchbook and journal.

"No ma'am, there's no property cataloged, but anything that may have been with her would have been left behind, having been soiled by …" and she continues somewhat unnecessarily, something about decomposition, the enclosed tent, the hot sun.

Arrangements are made at a San Diego crematorium, and I'm surprised to learn there is a wait list, at least two weeks before the funeral home can get to it. I tell them I want to be there when they do it, and that I will be bringing her ashes home with me. I make the flight arrangements for myself and James.

The next couple weeks go by in a fog. My mom helps me write an obituary, and I'm again surprised when told it'll be $500 to put an obit in the Sunday paper. I can't help thinking what a racket this death business is. A simple memorial is planned, to be held in our yard with its magnificent burr oaks. I hang my favorite photos of Shyloh from the ancient, far-reaching branches, having spent the entire week intimately moving each photo through my fingers, memories and tears pouring out of me as I paste them onto foam board and string them together. My hands work as Shyloh's had, wrapping stones and shells with copper wire, and I use these to weight her images against the wind, her smile flashing as the photos spin and sway.

GOING HOME – JULY 1, 2021

We are on our way to San Diego, to bring her home. I have a handful of memorial cards in my bag. The front of the card has one of Shyloh's senior pictures, my favorite, her head thrown back in laughter with that infectious toothy smile. On the back is the Dr. Seuss quote and Truffula tree. A good friend has also donated a handful of $25 McDonald's gift cards and I have these with me too, with the idea of giving them to the people in Shyloh's community.

The cremation is tomorrow. Weeks ago, both the Medical Examiner and the funeral home advised against me viewing her body, reminding me again – unnecessarily – of the circumstances. I agree passively but request to see a part of her, something identifiable. I mention her leg tattoo of the Truffula tree and Seuss quote, or maybe the sunflower tattoo on her shoulder, or the chameleon on her forearm, the Serenity prayer on her other arm. But as the day approaches my mind is swimming with agonizing visions of her death, and of the following days when she lay alone in that tent. My imaginings morph into horrors that I know will haunt

me for the rest of my life. And I know then with certainty
that as hard as it will be, I must witness her as she is before she's turned to ashes. I've witnessed every part of my
daughter's life, from the messiness of birth to her first broken heart, to her impossible life on the streets. I won't turn
away from her now. I call the funeral home and tell them I'll
be viewing her body after all, and I feel an inconceivable
peace with the decision.

I also have an intense need to see where she died and to
know what has happened to her things. The police give me
the location and, as I'd done so many times before, I pull
up Google maps and acquaint myself with the neighborhood.
I'm told that Shyloh's had been one among a short row of five
or six other tents, and Dalia, the woman who found Shyloh's
body, is called "Mom" by the folks in that community. I need
to find her too.

Our plane lands and we first head to our airbnb downtown,
a single bedroom cottage on a busy road just off the Interstate.
Homeless folks sleep huddled under blankets on every block.
A lot of them are in rough shape, clearly quite mentally ill and/
or strung out. It's an incredibly depressing sight, and I speculate as to why after the bus accident Shyloh hated the downtown area and refused to go near it anymore. I know she never
wanted to be seen as one of "them," viewing herself instead as
a free spirit having chosen to refuse conformity. I use the word
"homeless" here intentionally. Not all people living unhoused
are homeless. Shyloh had created several homes for herself
over these past few years living out on the streets. The people

we see here though, lying on the sidewalks up and down our block, have nothing resembling a home.

After dropping off our bags, we search for the spot where she died. We find the tent row easily. This mission feels so familiar: the pounding heart, the searching, the anticipation, and yet I have no words to describe how I feel as we walk towards these tents.

We find Mom's tent right away too. I call in through the flap. I'm greeted with suspicion but when I tell the small Latina woman that I'm Grace's – Shyloh's mom, her eyes well up and she comes over and hugs me. "You look like her," she says. I tell her I need to know what happened, what she knows, what she saw when she looked inside that tent, where Shyloh's things are.

Dalia tells me Grace had only been there about a week, that she'd been trying to get away from a new boyfriend who'd been beating up on her. I feel a simmering rage deep inside me. She tells me what a beautiful and loving spirit my daughter was. I nod. She tells me that she hadn't seen Grace for a couple days and then a terrible smell started coming from the tent. She tells me she can still smell it, that she'd said out loud, "Oh no, don't let it be her." She tells me the cops came and took Shyloh's body away, leaving everything else behind, that that's how the street people are treated, like roadkill, like garbage, like their lives mean nothing. I have witnessed this sentiment to some extent but had never felt it so viscerally before now. Dalia takes us over to where Shyloh's tent had been and shows us the memorial she made for her, a large stuffed animal, a white tiger, several wilted bouquets and a small rose bush in a pot that she tells me was Shyloh's. I am overcome with emotion by this, by the caring of this woman who had only known my daughter for a week.

I ask what happened to the tent, to Shyloh's things. The tent was tossed, Mom says, the smell was too awful, but she saved Shyloh's things for me, knowing intuitively that the child's mother would come for them eventually. Again I'm overwhelmed by this woman's compassion. She shows me Shyloh's bike, the one she bought that day when she called me from Goodwill. Mom tries to give it to me, but I tell her to keep it, or sell it, that I can't take it back with me on the plane. She goes behind her tent and comes back with a black garbage bag, hands it to me. James stands quietly, his arm protectively around me as I open it. There's a backpack and a plastic grocery bag inside, and a sickly-sweet odor that I know to be death. Instead of being repulsed by it, though, I'm oddly drawn to the smell.

I give Dalia a memorial card and several of the McDonald's gift cards, and she hugs me again.

We stop at the small bay park where I'd first met John and Georgia. They had heard the news already and I give them each a handful of cards. There are tears in John's eyes as he gets on his bike, and Georgia says, more to herself than to me, "Well, she's better off now. Who wants to live like this anyway."

I sit alone on the front porch of our airbnb and carefully open the bag again. I take each of her things out and handle them slowly, gently. The moment feels fragile somehow. I recognize the finality of it and I try to cherish each second.

There's a nearly empty photo album with a few doodles on the first page. Shyloh told me that day when she called from Goodwill that her journal and sketchbook had been stolen along with her bike. I suspect she bought this journal that day too. There's a small travel sewing kit, a first aid kit, a pocket knife, a small leather tool kit for hanging on a belt with a couple wrenches and other bike tools. There are several paint markers, pencils and pens, a few lighters, a half used roll of duct tape, a roll of electrical tape, a couple jars of nail polish and an eyeliner pencil, deodorant, toothbrush, a hairbrush, a baseball cap, a long-sleeved shirt, a broken phone and charger, a small box with some coins, a few AA batteries, a miniature beading kit with a small tangle of copper wire. Carefully, I put it all back into the bag.

I return to her things several times that day, turning them over in my hands. James runs the backpack and anything else washable through the laundry several times so I can bring them home. I'm reluctant to let go of any of it.

I take James to the nature reserve where I'd gone for so many cathartic runs. We go to dinner at the restaurant Shyloh and I had decided would become our traditional spot. And we walk. We walk for miles. We go to the beaches and parks I visited with Shyloh, and I introduce him to some of the places she'd called home. We meet a couple who are living in the space Shyloh had once named Fort Unicorn, and I ask if they remember her from a couple years ago. "Oh, yea, I remember her. She had the most beautiful eyes." They ask, "Is she missing or something?" I tell them she died. The woman hugs me, and I give her a memorial card, give them each a McDonald's gift card.

July 2

The next morning we go to the funeral home. I recognize a similar feeling to this, the feeling I would have the day of a boxing match, of holding back the adrenaline, of the anticipation of an unknown, of not thinking, just doing. This is so obviously different, but still, I know how to do it, how to put one foot in front of the other and walk up to the cardboard box that holds my daughter's body, to stand and watch as the lid is lifted. The shroud is a lovely lavender and I think absurdly what a beautiful color it is. A plastic bag rests on her legs near her feet, with her red skater sneakers, and the clothes she'd been wearing when she died. I ask if I can have them, and the bag is set at my feet. The shroud is pulled away and I look into her face, deeply discolored, empty eye sockets, lips

frozen into a rounded, toothless "O," so obviously dead. I pull
back the rest of the shroud to uncover her legs and I touch
the Truffula tree on her calf. Tears stream down my face as I
run my hands over her body, over the chameleon on her forearm, the sunflower on her shoulder, the Serenity prayer on her
other arm. I touch her darkened cheek.

When I'm done, James gently suggests we leave the bag
of clothes with her body and I agree. We put the bag back
in its place near her feet, and the lid is replaced. The box is
lifted, then slid into the furnace. The woman asks me if I want
to turn the knob to start the fire. I do. I had imagined I'd be
able to watch as the fire took hold but this specialized furnace
has no windows and instead we sit and watch the controls as
the temperature rises. I'm surprised to learn it will take four
hours to reduce her thirty-three years to ash, and after an hour
we leave to get coffee and come back when it's over. The urn
I've picked out is made of wood and looks like a large book,
painted copper and turquoise, with white cherry blossoms.

We stop to visit Tyler, the young man who has been Shyloh's friend since she first started living on the streets here
four years ago. Bill has since died and sadly Tyler too will
find himself on the streets soon when the house he'd lived in
with Bill is sold. I know that Shyloh loved Tyler, and even
though he often struggled to be with her when she was at
her worst, he loved her too, would look out for her when he
could, and would let me know when he'd seen her and that
she was okay. We hug and I give him Shyloh's bike tools and
a memorial card, and a promise to stay in touch.

July 3

James and I will fly home tomorrow and we decide to spend our last day in the airbnb. I keep going through Shyloh's things. I decide to put the three working lighters out on the ledge along the sidewalk out front, wondering if someone might claim them. About half an hour later I look out the screen door and see a woman there checking if the lighters work.

I call out the door, yes, please take them! She gets defensive and starts to leave, thinking I'm being sarcastic. No, no, please, wait?

She is tall and excruciatingly thin, missing most of her teeth, maybe Shyloh's age though it's hard to guess. She's pushing a shopping cart piled high with bags, and it appears she's been out here on the streets for a while. I ask the woman her name. "Catherine." I give her one of Shyloh's memorial cards, and I tell her about my daughter. She asks if she can hug me, then continues down the street with her new lighters and several McDonald's gift cards.

I consider that I could keep Shyloh's things, memorialized in a box in my closet, but I sense a connection with my daughter's generous spirit in sharing her few belongings with people who will use them. I put the sewing kit and electrical tape out on the ledge, and they are gone in another few minutes.

I don't give everything away. I choose to keep the backpack and photo album, the paint markers and bead kit, the shirt, the hairbrush, the hat. But I put the rest of it on the ledge with a note saying, "Free – Please take it if you can use it."

All of it is taken.

July 4

Going through security is the last piece of this trip that I need to gather my courage for. I am grateful for the mandatory masks that cover my contorting face as the tears flow unchecked. Again my heart is pounding, but this time I don't know how to continue. I have run out of courage. My hands and voice are shaking. I say, "I have these ashes ..."

They don't understand what I'm saying and mercifully James steps up and explains that I'm holding my daughter's cremains. They gently take the urn and run it through separately from everything else, then wipe it down, looking for explosive residues. When it's handed back to me, I carefully return it to my backpack and we head to the gate.

I watch San Diego pull away through the plane's small window, Shyloh's ashes tucked carefully away beneath the seat in front of me. We are going home.

AFTER – JANUARY 2022

James and I are heading downtown with a large box of winter socks and several large packs of hand warmers. It's especially cold this morning when we leave the house, in the negative single digits, and I have only a vague idea of searching for the people in need of these small but necessary comforts. We drive to a park that in warmer weather I know to be regularly occupied, but unlike San Diego, an unhoused person in this weather would soon freeze to death. I'm relieved to see the park empty.

I pull up a list of local shelters and warming houses and start calling. The only person who answers any of my calls is the receptionist at a warming house and resource center for people living homeless with mental illness. I ask her if they have a use for my offerings, if I could bring them by now. "Oh yes, absolutely!" she exclaims.

The warm lobby at Safe Haven is full, men and women lounging on plastic chairs, bundled in coats and boots, a few animated discussions here and there, and a television blaring in the corner.

As I climb back into the car after having completed this small mission, I am struck by how oddly simple it was.

It's been seven months since Shyloh died, and in a way I feel as though I've been practicing for this grief for the past five years. The void left in my center is so bottomless and un-like anything I've ever experienced. I know with a certainty as absolute as my love for her that it will stay with me until I die. I had a memorial tattoo done yesterday, by the owner of the tattoo shop where Shyloh worked doing piercings when she lived here in Madison. She would've been tickled by this. The tattoo has sunflowers and bear tracks and a dragonfly, and I feel a strange full circle-ness to the deed.

I dreamt the other night that her hand was in mine. I kept saying "I'm sorry, I'm sorry, I'm sorry," for what exactly I can't articulate. "It's okay, Mama," was the disembodied re-ply. It felt so incredibly real. I could still feel her touch when I woke, my pillow tear-soaked, to find my own hand resting in the palm of the other.

Last night a winter storm with sixty-five-plus mile-per-hour gusts toppled vulnerable trees and power lines. By sun-rise the winds have calmed, and I go out to check the photos of Shyloh hanging from the oak's branches. This morning most of them lie strewn about the grass; the few that have held tight are wrapped in tangles among the branches. Each time I retrieve one from the grass, I resist the sharp stabbing sense of loss it brings to see it lying there untethered, and the wave of grief that I know will follow. I gather them up and take them inside, wipe them off, and retie the loops. Back outside, I string them up again and untangle the others from high in the tree. I'm torn by the desperate desire to keep them hanging there, swinging freely in the wind and sun and rain as they are, protected forever, and the simultaneous knowledge that it is ultimately, obviously, a futile endeavor. And yet I am compelled to keep repairing and rehanging them, and then once they've been put in order I will sit futilely in the small wooden chair at the edge of the yard with a fleeting sense of something resembling contentment, and watch her images again dance and twist in the breeze.

Shyloh, 3 years old

Shyloh showing her typical dramatic flair

Letter to teenage self

ShyShy! Hey Girlie, I am hoping you get this in good health... I know things have been rough but if you could only see how strong you are. The road ahead of you is not an easy one man, I made it real hard for us- by putting my faith and loyalty and trust in all the wrong people, for all the wrong reasons. The true person to show your well of love and passion to? Is yourself. Still, today, at 30 yrs old, we aren't so great at that part. Don't worry about being accepted by the "right" crowd. Turns out we have a unique ability of shaping those around us so JUST BE YOU. You're a smart, vibrant, beautiful young woman, and too often do you allow the demons you battle to win. The path is set, but advice to make it easier? Do what you love, fuck the fakes and the burnouts. Be in nature; write, draw. The moments you second guess? Worry about missing out? There will always be another party, mission, drink or drug, but you won't always have your family to hug. Don't let yourself down by fading away. Hold your head high and just TRY. Try every day.

Love ya bitchface!! =) LB

ACKNOWLEDGEMENTS

A thank you to Connections Counseling and to FLYY for giving Shyloh your love and support when she was able to ask for and accept it.

Thank you to Orange Hat's art director, Kaeley Dunteman, for your artistic expertise in helping me create the beautiful cover designs, and to my Orange Hat editor, Pam Parker, for your thoughtful suggestions and edits. It's been such a pleasure working with you.

Thank you, Mom, for your loving support and keen editor's eye, and dear friends Renee, Jennifer, and Clare, for being there without question when I needed you most. Thank you, cousin Kathy, for patiently guiding me as I floundered.

Thank you, Kristina, for your gift of time and endless support, giving your talent toward putting voice to my written words.

And a special thanks to Matt, my cheerleader, editor, and friend. Thank you for putting up with my impatience and compulsive drive, for encouraging me and offering guidance, and for all the hours you put into helping me tell Shyloh's story as beautifully as I could.

I am so lucky to have such good friends.

And of course, thank you James, for being my rock. I would be lost without you.

ABOUT THE AUTHOR

Andrea Nelson lives and coaches boxing in Madison, Wisconsin. When she's not in the gym training her boxers, you can find Andrea out tending her gardens, chickens, and bees, or running the nearby trails. She shares life with her partner, James.

CPSIA information can be obtained
at www.ICGtesting.com
Printed in the USA
BVHW081734260922
647884BV00005B/17

9 781645 384250